ESSENTIAL
Crochet
DICTIONARY

Essential Crochet Dictionary

Landauer Publishing, www.landauerpub.com, is an imprint of Fox Chapel Publishing Company, Inc.

L'essentiel des points de crochet © 2016, 2022, Éditions Eyrolles, Paris, France

English translation, *Essential Crochet Dictionary*, © 2024 Fox Chapel Publishing Company, Inc.

Essential Crochet Dictionary is an translation of the 2022 version originally published in French by Éditions Eyrolles under the title *L'essentiel des points de crochet* in Paris, France. This version is published by Landaur, an imprint of Fox Chapel Publishing Company, Inc.

Éditions Eyrolles Team
Editorial Director: Claire Rius
Art Director: Charles Buxin
Photography: Étienne Galopin

Fox Chapel Publishing Team
Managing Editor: Gretchen Bacon
Acquisitions Editor: Amelia Johanson
Translator: Heather Carroll
Tech Editor: Rita Greenfeder
Copy Editor: Christa Oestreich
Designer: Freire Disseny + Comunicació

ISBN 978-1-63981-099-4

Library of Congress Control Number: 2024910237

To learn more about the other great books from Fox Chapel Publishing, or to find a retailer near you, call toll-free 800-457-9112, send mail to 903 Square Street, Mount Joy, PA 17552, or visit us at www.FoxChapelPublishing.com.
We are always looking for talented authors. To submit an idea, please send a brief inquiry to acquisitions@foxchapelpublishing.com.

Printed in China
First printing

ESSENTIAL
Crochet
DICTIONARY

A Visual Guide to Stitches and Techniques

Sophie Martin

Landauer Publishing

Contents

Getting Started

Terms Used

ARC OR ARCH

◄ Chain stitches form an arc or arch which, in the next row, provides support for other stitches. For this, the hook is hooked under the arch. The arc can be more or less rounded, depending on the ratio between the number of chain stitches and the number of skipped stitches.

BORDER

This is a crochet pattern used to decorate the edge of a crocheted or knitted item. For the latter, the stitches are bound off using slip stitches. Examples found on pages 138–159.

CHAIN STITCH

◄ Abbreviated as **ch**, a chain stitch is made without inserting the hook under a top stitch. It can be used to restore the row height at the beginning of a row (chain stitch for turning). If so, it is not included in the pattern stitches. The first stitch in the row always begins after the turning chain stitch(es).

DECREASE

◄ The most common way of doing this is to skip the stitches you'd like to reduce at the end of a row. For a single crochet piece, start the row with slip stitches over the number of stitches to be reduced. To achieve a rounded reduction on a row of double crochet stitches, use a slip stitch, a single crochet, and a half double crochet in succession over the stitches to be reduced.

DOUBLE CROCHET

▶ Abbreviated as **dc**, the double crochet is one of the basic stitches.

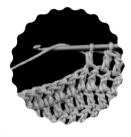

DOUBLE TREBLE CROCHET

Abbreviated as **dtr**, the double treble crochet is one of the basic stitches (see page 23).

DRAW THROUGH LOOPS

◀ This expression is used when you have several loops or stitches on your hook. The yarn from a yarn over is pulled through. For certain relief stitches, several stitches may be drawn together.

Table of Chain Stitches for Turning

The number of chain stitches required for turning depends on the height of the stitch used to make the first chain stitch in the row. This number is usually indicated at the beginning of the row. The table below shows the quantities needed for basic stitches.

slip stitch: 1 chain stitch
single crochet: 1 chain stitch
extended single crochet: 2 chain stitches
half double crochet: 2 chain stitches
double crochet: 3 chain stitches
treble crochet: 4 chain stitches
double treble crochet: 5 chain stitches

EXTENDED SINGLE CROCHET

Abbreviated as **esc**, the extended single crochet is one of the basic stitches (see page 17).

FORWARD AND RETURN

◄ The term "forward" is used in Tunisian crochet to refer to the row running from right to left on the piece. On the forward pass, the stitches are kept on the hook. ◄ On the return pass, i.e. from left to right, they are drawn through.

FRONT AND BACK LOOPS

◄ The top stitch is made up of two loops. The one at the front is called the "front loop," ▲ while the one behind is called the "back loop." Inserting the hook through either loop creates a small line on the opposite row. Some patterns, such as the Albanian stitch (see page 32), make use of this effect.

HALF DOUBLE CROCHET

◄ Abbreviated as **hdc**, the half double crochet is one of the basic stitches.

FOUNDATION CHAIN

◄ The foundation chain is made up of a sequence of chain stitches; it's the starting point for all stitches, including in Tunisian crochet. The pattern explanations start at the first row, assuming that a foundation chain has already been made (see page 8).

INCREASE

▲ Stitch increases are quite subtle. They are achieved by inserting the hook into the same stitch twice, preferably at the end of a row. To keep track of increases, we recommend marking them with colored yarn. To increase the number of stitches, add chain stitches at the end of the row.

LONG LOOPS

◄ Long yarn overs can form long loops. On a row of single crochet stitches, wrap the yarn around a thick or thin needle (depending on the size of loop you want) as you make a stitch. Once the row is complete, you can cut the loops to create a fur-like texture.

LONG STITCH

▶ Inserting the hook under one or more previous rows, rather than under the top stitch, lengthens the stitch.

LOOP OR STITCH

The term "loop" or "stitch" is used to refer to the stitch actually on the hook; it may be the result of the yarn over passing through one or more other stitches. When the loops are "drawn through," the thread passes through them, and they are no longer on the hook.

MESH OR NETTING

The mesh design is a set of very loose stitches that can be used as the base for other decorative stitches. Examples found on pages 70–85.

NUMBER OF STITCHES

Indicated for each different stitch, the number of individual stitches can be "any" or multiples of a number. One or more individual stitches can be added at the beginning or end of the row to complete the pattern.

PICOT

◄ The picot is a small tooth made from chain stitches, joined at the base by a slip stitch.

SCALLOP

◄ When several double crochets (made in either a stitch or an arch) are tightened together, they form a scallop.

PULL A LOOP

► After one yarn over, the yarn is pulled through a stitch, forming a new loop.

SELVAGE STITCH

When chain stitches are used for turning, they can create a selvage. On the other hand, additional stitches (indicated as additional to the pattern stitches) are sometimes required to complete a pattern.

SINGLE CROCHET

► Abbreviated as sc, the single crochet is one of the basic stitches.

RELIEF STITCH

◄ Inserting the hook under a stitch in the previous row, rather than under the top stitch, shifts the row and creates a relief.

SKIP STITCHES

Some stitches require you to skip one or more top stitches. For example, when three stitches are skipped, the hook is inserted into every fourth top stitch.

SLIP STITCH

Abbreviated as sl st, the slip stitch involves inserting the hook, making one yarn over, and drawing the yarn through the two loops. This inconspicuous stitch is used to hold picots in place. For when several stitches are drawn through together, see Draw Through Loops (page 9).

TOP STITCH

▼ Once completed, a row is made up of top stitches under which the hook can be inserted to create the next row. Each top stitch is made up of two loops: front and back.

TREBLE CROCHET

◄ Abbreviated as tr, the treble crochet is one of the basic stitches.

TRIM

◄ Made with just a few rows (one to four), a trim is a narrow strip sewn onto a piece of fabric. A trim can decorate the edge or any other part of a piece

YARN OVER

▼ The yarn over consists of wrapping the yarn around the hook to form a new stitch. Depending on the stitch, one or more yarn overs can be performed.

Abbreviations Used

To save time when reading, most crochet instructions use abbreviations. Use this handy reminder to keep yourself on track.

...: repeat the steps between the asterisks
ch: chain stitch
dc: double crochet
dtr: double treble crochet
esc: extended single crochet
hdc: half double crochet
nxt: next
prev: previous
rw: row
sc: single crochet
sl st: slip stitch
st(s): stitch(es)
tog: together
tr: treble crochet

Foundation Chain

This is the starting row for all stitches. The foundation chain owes its name to the series of small stitches that look like a chain.

EQUIPMENT

- crochet hook
- yarn

USES

- the starting row for all stitches

1▲ Place the yarn across the hook, leaving a short end of about 4" (10.2cm).

2▲ Wrap it around the hook once and pull the yarn through the loop. You'll then have a first loop. Hold the short end of the yarn with the hand that's holding the hook.

3▲ Pass the other end of the yarn around the hook. Using the tip of the hook, pull the yarn through the loop. You've made your first stitch.

Tip

To make sure your chain is even, don't tighten the yarn, as this makes it difficult to insert the hook into each stitch.

4▶ To form a new stitch, wrap the yarn around the hook, and pull it through the loop formed by the first stitch.

Single and Extended Single Crochet

These compact stitches, made up of two or three yarn overs, form the basis of many decorative stitches.

EQUIPMENT

- crochet hook
- yarn

USES

- basic stitch

ABBREVIATIONS

- sc (single crochet)
- esc (extended single crochet)

SINGLE CROCHET

Number of Stitches: any
Row 1: 1 ch to turn, *insert under top stitch, 1 yarn over, pull 1 loop, 1 yarn over, pull yarn through 2 loops* Repeat this row as many times as needed.

TECHNIQUE

1▼ Insert the hook under the top stitch and do 1 yarn over.

2▲ Pull the yarn through the top stitch. You'll now have 2 loops on your hook.
3▼ Yarn over once more.

4▲ Pull the yarn through the 2 loops. You'll be left with 1 stitch on your hook.

EXTENDED SINGLE CROCHET

1. In contrast to the single crochet stitch, the extended single crochet has 1 extra yarn over and uses 2 chain stitches to turn.
2. Do steps 1 and 2 the same as single crochet. Add an extra yarn over and pull the yarn through the loop. You'll now have 2 loops on your hook. Continue with steps 3 and 4.

Half Double Crochet

Halfway between the single and double crochet stitches, the half double crochet is produced using three yarn overs.

EQUIPMENT

- crochet hook
- yarn

USES

- basic stitch

ABBREVIATION

- hdc (half double crochet)

THE STITCH

Number of Stitches: any
Row 1: 2 ch to turn, *1 yarn over, insert hook under top stitch, 1 yarn over, pull 1 loop, 1 yarn over, pull yarn through the 3 remaining loops* Repeat this row as many times as needed.

TECHNIQUE

1▼ Yarn over once and insert the hook under the top stitch.

2▼ Yarn over again and thread the yarn through the top stitch. You'll be left with 3 stitches on your hook.

3▼ Do 1 final yarn over and thread the yarn through the 3 stitches. You'll be left with 1 stitch on your hook.

Tip

The half double crochet can also be produced by inserting the hook under the top stitch's front or back loop, like in the Albanian stitch (see page 32).

¤

Double Crochet

This stitch is made in four stages, representing the number of times a yarn over is passed through the loops.

EQUIPMENT
- crochet hook
- yarn

USES
- basic stitch

ABBREVIATION
- dc (double crochet)

THE STITCH

Number of Stitches: any

Row 1: 3 ch to turn, *1 yarn over, insert hook under top stitch, 1 yarn over, pull 1 loop, 1 yarn over, pull yarn through 2 loops, 1 yarn over, pull yarn through the 2 remaining loops*
Repeat this row as many times as needed.

TECHNIQUE

1▾ Yarn over once and insert the hook under the top stitch.

2▴ Yarn over again and thread the yarn through the top stitch. You'll be left with 3 stitches on your hook.

3▾ Yarn over a 3rd time and thread the yarn through the 2 stitches. You'll be left with 2 stitches on your hook.

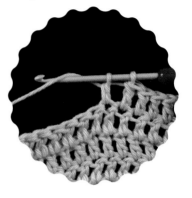

4. Do 1 final yarn over and thread the yarn through the 2 loops.

Tip

You will need to make three chain stitches to turn in order to match the level of the double crochet in the next row.

¤

Treble and Double Treble Crochet

Depending on the number of yarn overs at the beginning of the stitch, you'll produce a treble crochet (two yarn overs) or a double treble crochet (three yarn overs).

EQUIPMENT

- crochet hook
- yarn

USES

- basic stitch

ABBREVIATIONS

- tr (treble crochet)
- dtr (double treble crochet)

TREBLE CROCHET

Number of Stitches: any
Row 1: 4 ch for turning, *2 yarn overs, insert under the top stitch, 1 yarn over, pull 1 loop, 1 yarn over, pull yarn through 2 loops, 1 yarn over, pull yarn through 2 loops, 1 yarn over, pull yarn through the remaining 2 loops*
Repeat this row as many times as needed.

TECHNIQUE

1▼ Yarn over twice and insert the hook under the top stitch.

2. Yarn over again and thread the yarn through the top stitch. You'll be left with 4 stitches on your hook.

3. Yarn over a 4th time and thread the yarn through the 2 stitches. You'll be left with 3 stitches on your hook.

4▲ Yarn over a 5th time and thread the yarn through the 2 stitches. You'll be left with 2 stitches on your hook.

5. Do a final yarn over and thread the yarn through the remaining 2 stitches. You'll be left with 1 stitch on your hook.

DOUBLE TREBLE CROCHET

Number of Stitches: any
Row 1: 5 ch to turn, *3 yarn overs, insert under top stitch, 1 yarn over, pull 1 loop, x4 (1 yarn over, pull yarn through 2 loops)*
Repeat this row as many times as needed.

Tip

For orientation, once the loop has been pulled through the top stitch, the stitches are threaded in pairs until the last step.

¤

Tunisian Crochet

Tunisian crochet is a special crochet technique in which the stitches are retained on a long hook.

EQUIPMENT

- Tunisian crochet hook
- yarn

USES

- basic technique

STITCH USED

- Tunisian simple stitch

1▲ Create a foundation chain with the desired number of stitches. Make 1 extra chain stitch to turn.

2▲ The first forward row runs from right to left. Insert the hook under the top stitch, do 1 yarn over, and pull through 1 loop, repeating the process for the whole row, leaving the pulled-through loops on the hook. The thread remains behind.

3▲ At the end of the row, make 1 chain stitch for the return. This is done from left to right, without turning the piece. Yarn over once and thread the yarn through 2 loops, repeating the process for the entire row. Simple stitch return rows are always done identically.

Tip

Tunisian crochet alternates between forward and return rows. For the forward pass, the stitches are kept on the hook, while on the return pass, they are drawn through.

¤

Full Stitches

Lemon Peel Stitch

Alternating double and single crochet stitches give this pattern a slightly gritty look.

EQUIPMENT

- crochet hook
- yarn

USES

- accessories
- borders
- main body

STITCHES USED

- single crochet
- double crochet

THE STITCH

Number of Stitches: pairs
Row 1: 1 ch to turn, *1 sc, 1 dc*
Repeat this row as many times as needed.

TECHNIQUE

1. Make 1 chain stitch to turn.
2 ▼ Insert the hook under the top stitch and make 1 single crochet.

3 ▲ Yarn over once and insert the hook under the top stitch to make 1 double crochet stitch.

4. Repeat steps 2 and 3 to the end of the row.

DOUBLE LEMON PEEL STITCH

Number of Stitches: any
Row 1: 2 ch to turn, *1 esc, 1 sc, skip 1 st*
Row 2: 2 ch to turn, *1 esc by inserting under the ch of the prev rw, 1 ch, skip 1 st*
After rows 1 and 2, keep repeating row 2.

TECHNIQUE

1. Insert the hook under the top stitch, 1 yarn over, pull 1 loop, 1 yarn over, pull 1 loop, 1 yarn over, pull the yarn through the remaining 2 stitches.

Tip

For orientation, the single and double crochets in each row are offset from the previous row.

¤

Wattle Stitch

The imbalance between the single and double crochet stitches creates little wreaths, arranged in a staggered formation.

EQUIPMENT
- crochet hook
- yarn

USES
- sleeve edges
- borders
- main body

STITCHES USED
- single crochet
- double crochet
- half double crochet

THE STITCH

Number of Stitches: multiples of 3
Row 1: 2 ch to turn, 1 hdc, skip 1 st, *1 sc, 1 ch, 1 dc, skip 2 st,* 1 sc
Row 2: 2 ch to turn, 1 hdc, skip 1 st, *under each ch (1 sc, 1 ch, 1 dc), skip 2 st,* 1 sc under the 2 selvage ch
After rows 1 and 2, keep repeating row 2.

Tip

For orientation, the chain stitch is located in the middle of the design and not where two designs meet, at which point the stitch is stretched out.

¤

TECHNIQUE

1▼ In the second and subsequent rows, the chain stitches from the previous row are used to support the new group of stitches. Insert the hook under each of them and make 1 single crochet . . .

2. . . . 1 chain stitch ▲ and 1 double crochet ▼. Skip 2 stitches and begin again in the subsequent chain stitch.

Albanian Stitch

This striped stitch is made up of single crochets drawn from the top stitch's front or back loops.

EQUIPMENT

- crochet hook
- yarn

USES

- borders
- main body

STITCH USED

- single crochet

THE STITCH

Number of Stitches: any
Row 1: 1 ch to turn, sc for the rest of the rw
Row 2: 1 ch to turn, sc for the rest of the rw, by inserting under the top stitch's back loop
Row 3: 1 ch to turn, sc for the rest of the rw, by inserting under the top stitch's front loop
After rows 1 and 3, keep repeating rows 2 and 3.

Tip

For orientation, the single crochets inserted under the front loop form a line of small oblique stitches, while those inserted under the back loop form a line of small horizontal stitches.

¤

TECHNIQUE

1. For row 1, make 1 chain stitch to turn, and then single crochets for the rest of the row.

2▲ For row 2, make 1 chain stitch to turn. To make the single crochets, insert the hook under the back loop (the one behind).

3▲ For row 3, make 1 chain stitch to turn. To make the single crochets, insert the hook under the top stitch's front loop (i.e. the one in front) rather than under the top stitch itself.

Slanting Squares Stitch

Oriented either to the left or to the right, the groups of double crochets look like little squares.

EQUIPMENT

- crochet hook
- yarn

USES

- borders
- main body

STITCHES USED

- single crochet
- double crochet
- chain stitch

THE STITCH

Number of Stitches: multiples of 4 sts +3

Row 1: 3 ch to turn, *2 dc, in 1 single st (1 dc, 3 ch, 1 sc), skip 1 st,* 3 dc

Row 2: 2 ch to turn, *under the ch of the prev rw (3 dc, 3 ch, 1 sc),* 1 dc under the selvage ch

After rows 1 and 2, keep repeating row 2.

TECHNIQUE

1▼ Row 1 is a preparation for the following rows. Make 3 chain stitches to turn and repeat the following: 2 double crochets, in 1 stitch make 1 double crochet, 3 chain stitches, and 1 single crochet, then skip 1 stitch. Finish the row with 3 double crochets.

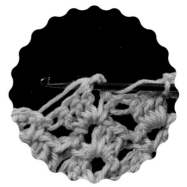

2. For row 2 onward, make 2 chain stitches to turn. Inserting the hook under the chain stitches in the previous row, make 3 double crochets ▲, 3 chain stitches, and 1 single crochet. Finish the row with 1 double crochet, inserting the hook under the selvage stitches.

Tip

For orientation, groups of three double crochets are staggered and attached to the three chain stitches in the previous row.

¤

Cross Stitch

The crossover is made by inserting the hook under two successive top stitches and retaining the stitches.

EQUIPMENT

- crochet hook
- yarn

USES

- accessories
- main body

STITCHES USED

- double crochet
- chain stitch

THE STITCH

Number of Stitches: pairs

Row 1: 3 ch, *1 yarn over, insert under top stitch, 1 yarn over, pull 1 loop, 1 yarn over, insert under nxt st, 1 yarn over, pull 1 loop, 1 yarn over, draw through all 5 loops, 1 ch*

Row 2: 3 ch to turn, *1 yarn over, insert hook under the ch in the prev rw, 1 yarn over, pull 1 loop, 1 yarn over, insert hook under the nxt ch, 1 yarn over, pull 1 loop, 1 yarn over, draw through the 5 loops, 1 ch ,* 1 dc
After rows 1 and 2, keep repeating row 2.

TECHNIQUE

1. Row 1 is a preparation for the following rows. It's made up of half double crochets and chain stitches. These serve as a support (the hook is inserted underneath them) for the next row's half double crochets.

2▼ In row 2, make 3 chain stitches to turn, then 1 yarn over and insert the hook under the chain stitch in the previous row. Yarn over once and pull through a stitch.

3▲ Yarn over again, then insert the hook under the next chain stitch.

4▼ Yarn over once more, pull through a stitch, and yarn over again, then thread the yarn through the 5 stitches on the hook.

Tip

To make it easier to insert the hook under the loops, especially the last five stitches, avoid pulling the yarn overs too tightly.

¤

Rosette Stitch

This decorative, lacy crochet design is created by combining various stitches.

EQUIPMENT

- crochet hook
- yarn

USES

- accessories
- borders
- main body

STITCHES USED

- single crochet
- chain stitch
- half double crochet

THE STITCH

Number of Stitches: multiples of 2 sts +6

Row 1: ch to turn, 1 sc, 4 sc joined tog without drawing through the last loop, 1 ch, *4 sc joined tog (the 1st inserted under the prev ch, the 2nd under the last sc), 1 ch,* 1 hdc

Row 2: ch to turn, *2 hdc under the st joining the sc,* 1 hdc

Repeat these two rows as many times as needed.

Tip

For orientation, the double crochets in the second radiate out from the center to complete the rosettes.

¤

TECHNIQUE

1▼ Make 1 chain stitch to turn and 1 single crochet. To make the single crochets joined together, insert the hook under the top stitch, yarn over once, and pull through 1 loop. Repeat 3 times. You'll be left with 5 stitches on your hook. Yarn over and thread the yarn through the 5 stitches. Make 1 chain stitch.

2. Repeat the following steps: Make 4 single crochets joined together. Insert the first stitch under the previous ch, the second under the last single crochet ▲, then the other 2 under the subsequent top stitches. Add 1 chain stitch. Finish the row with 1 half double crochet.

3. For row 2, make 2 chain stitches to turn and 2 half double crochets by inserting the hook into the center of the combined stitches to form the rosette. Finish the row with 1 half double crochet.

Arch Stitch

A scallop of double crochets decorates the arches, enhancing their natural curvature.

EQUIPMENT

- crochet hook
- yarn

USES

- accessories
- main body

STITCHES USED

- single crochet
- double crochet
- chain stitch

THE STITCH

Number of Stitches: multiples of 6 sts +1

Row 1: 1 ch, 1 sc, *3 ch, skip 3 sts, 3 sc,* 3 ch, 2 sc

Row 2: 1 ch to turn, *skip 1 st, 5 dc under the 3 ch on the prev rw, skip 1 st, 1 sc,* 1 sc

Row 3: 3 ch to turn, skip 2 sts, *3 sc, 3 ch, skip 3 sts,* 3 sc, 2 ch, skip 1 st, 1 sc

Row 4: 3 ch to turn, skip 1 st, 2 dc by inserting hook under the ch in the prev rw, *skip 1 st, 1 sc, skip 1 st, 5 dc in the 3 ch in the prev rw,* skip 1 st, 1 sc, skip 1 st, 2 dc under the 3 ch in the prev rw

Row 5: 1 ch to turn, skip 1 st, 1 sc, *3 ch, skip 3 sts, 3 sc,* 2 sc

After the first 5 rows, keep repeating rows 2–5.

TECHNIQUE

1▼ In rows 2 and 4, the double crochets forming the arch scallop are grouped in fives by inserting the crochet hook under the 3 chain stitches in the previous row.

2▲ In rows 3 and 5, the arches are formed by 3 chain stitches that connect the double crochet scallops in the previous row. The arches are separated by 3 single crochets.

Tip

For orientation, the single crochets in rows 3 and 5 are made on the second, third, and fourth double crochets in the previous row, while the first and fifth double crochets are skipped.

¤

Judith Stitch

A long stitch encircling a group of four double crochets gives this design the appearance of a twisted rib.

EQUIPMENT
- crochet hook
- yarn

USES
- borders
- main body

STITCHES USED
- single crochet
- double crochet
- long stitch

THE STITCH

Number of Stitches: multiples of 4 sts +2

Row 1: 1 ch to turn, sc for the rest of the row

Row 2: 2 ch to turn, *skip 1 st, 3 dc, 1 sc inserted under the skipped st,* 1 dc Repeat these two rows as many times as needed.

TECHNIQUE

1. Make a row of single crochets, inserting the hook under the top stitch.

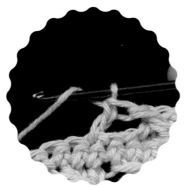

2.▲ For row 2, make 2 chain stitches to turn. Skip 1 stitch, and make 1 double crochet in each of the next 3 stitches.

3. Insert the hook under the top stitch of the skipped stitch ▲, making a single crochet. Yarn over and pull through 1 long loop, yarn over again ▼, and draw through the 2 stitches.

Tip

The group of three double crochets must be passed diagonally through the long stitch. Make sure you don't pull the loop too tight.

¤

Braided Stitch

The long stitches that cut across rows have been given a variety of colorful names: "tall stitch" or "spike stitch."

EQUIPMENT

- crochet hook
- yarn

USES

- accessories
- main body

STITCHES USED

- single crochet
- long stitch

ESSENTIAL CROCHET DICTIONARY

THE STITCH

Number of Stitches: multiples of 4 sts
Row 1: 1 ch to turn, the rest like the
Albanian stitch (see page 32)
Row 2: 1 ch to turn, *3 sc, 1 long st
inserted under the prev rw*
Repeat these two rows as many
times as needed. To stagger the long
stitches, start row 2 with 1 single
crochet.

VARIANT

In row 1, use the back loop to enhance
the relief effect of the stitch. This row
is then the right side of the piece. If
you use the front loop, row 1 will be
the wrong side of the piece.

TECHNIQUE

1▼ Make a chain stitch to turn and
then the rest of the row with
single crochets inserted under
the front loop of the top stitch.

2▲ In row 2, the long stitches are
single crochet stitches made by
inserting the hook under the
previous row. The yarn in the
first loop is lengthened to the
level of the row.

Tip

Each long stitch is separated
from the next one by three single
crochets, so don't forget to skip
the top stitch associated with it.

✶

Open Diamond Stitch

This stitch gets its name from its perfect lines, which make it a very dainty design.

EQUIPMENT

- crochet hook
- yarn

USES

- accessories
- borders
- main body

STITCHES USED

- single crochet
- double crochet
- chain stitch

THE STITCH

Number of Stitches: pairs
Row 1: 1 ch to turn, sc for the rest of the rw
Row 2: 3 ch to turn, *1 yarn over, insert hook under the top stitch, 1 yarn over, pull 1 loop, 1 yarn over, insert hook under nxt st, 1 yarn over, pull 1 loop, 1 yarn over, draw through the 5 loops, 1 ch*
Repeat these two rows as many times as needed.

VARIANT

For a more open design, space the double crochets further apart using 2 chain stitches and 1 skipped stitch.

TECHNIQUE

1. For row 1, make 1 chain stitch to turn and then continue with single crochets for the rest of the row.
2▼ For row 2, make 3 chain stitches to turn, then repeat the following steps: 1 yarn over, insert the hook under the top stitch, 1 yarn over, pull 1 loop, 1 yarn over, and insert the hook under the next top stitch.

3▲ Yarn over once, pull 1 loop, and then yarn over again. There will be 6 stitches on your hook. Pull the yarn through 5 stitches. Separate each of the double crochets that follow with 1 chain stitch.

Tip

For orientation, the double crochets are made on two top stitches and must be aligned vertically.

¤

Star Stitch

*The set of double crochets creates
a distinctive star pattern.*

EQUIPMENT

- crochet hook
- yarn

USES

- accessories
- borders
- collars
- main body

STITCH USED

- double crochet

THE STITCH

Number of Stitches: multiples of 3
Row 1: 2 ch to turn, 1 dc, *1 dc inserted into the same st, 1 yarn over, insert hook into the same st, 1 yarn over, pull 1 loop, 1 yarn over, draw through 2 loops, 1 yarn over, skip 1 st, insert hook into nxt st, 1 yarn over, draw through 1 loop, 1 yarn over, draw through 2 loops, 1 yarn over, draw through 3 loops*
Repeat this row as many times as needed.

Tip

For orientation, the groups of three double crochets are aligned vertically. At the end of the pattern, a new double crochet is detached, and the next double crochet is made in it.

¤

TECHNIQUE

1▼ Make 2 chain stitches to turn and a double crochet, then repeat the following steps: In the same stitch as the previous double crochet, make 1 double crochet, then yarn over and insert the hook into the same stitch once more. Yarn over again, pull a loop, yarn over once more, and pull 2 loops. There will be 2 loops on your hook, yarn over another time.

2▲ Skip 1 stitch and insert the hook into the next stitch. Yarn over once, pull 1 loop, yarn over again, pull 2 loops, yarn over again, and draw the yarn through the remaining 3 loops.

Pike Stitch

Made with two stitches, this design crosses the double crochets to create a subtle relief effect.

EQUIPMENT

- crochet hook
- yarn

USES

- borders
- main body

STITCHES USED

- single crochet
- double crochet

THE STITCH

Number of Stitches: pairs
Row 1: 2 ch to turn, 1 dc, *1 yarn over, insert hook into the same st, 1 yarn over, pull 1 loop, insert hook into nxt st, 1 yarn over, pull 1 loop, 1 yarn over, draw through 3 loops, 1 yarn over, draw through 2 loops*
Row 2: 1 ch to turn, sc for the rest of the rw
Repeat these two rows as many times as needed.

VARIANT

For a looser design, make 4 chain stitches to turn at the end of row 1, and replace the double crochet with a treble crochet. Start the stitch with 2 yarn overs, and finish by drawing through 3 loops.

TECHNIQUE

1▼ For row 1, make 2 chain stitches to turn and one double crochet, then repeat the following steps: 1 yarn over, insert the hook in the previous double crochet, 1 yarn over, and pull a loop. There will be 3 stitches on your hook.

2▲ Insert the hook into the next stitch, yarn over once, and pull a loop. There will be 4 stitches on your hook. Yarn over once and thread the yarn through 3 stitches. Do a final yarn over and thread the yarn through the remaining 2 loops.

Tip

This stitch has a different pattern on each side. For orientation, row 2 always starts on the side with the starting thread.

¤

Square Stitch

This stitch stacks double crochets together like toy blocks.

EQUIPMENT

- crochet hook
- yarn

USES

- accessories
- main body

STITCH USED

- double crochet

THE STITCH

Number of Stitches: pairs
Row 1: 3 ch to turn, *2 dc in the same st, skip 1 st,* 2 dc in the same st
Row 2: 3 ch to turn, *2 dc inserted between the dc groups in the prev rw,* 2 dc in the selvage st
After rows 1 and 2, keep repeating row 2.

VARIANT

For larger squares, make 3 double crochets instead of 2 in row 1, and skip 2 stitches. In row 2, make 3 double crochets between the groups of double crochets in the prev row.

TECHNIQUE

1▼ Make 3 chain stitches to turn. For the whole row, keep repeating 2 double crochets with the hook inserted into the same stitch, then skip 1 stitch. Finish with 2 double crochets in the last stitch.

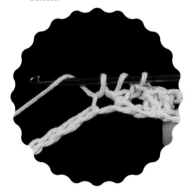

2▲ Make 3 chain stitches to turn, then complete the row with 2 double crochets between each group of chain stitches in the previous row. Finish the row with 2 double crochets in the selvage stitch.

Tip

In row 2, insert the crochet hook in the space created by the skipped stitch that separates the groups of 2 double crochets.

¤

Palm Stitch

This stitch is inspired by the small, stylized palm leaves arranged in a fan shape that is found in architecture.

EQUIPMENT

- crochet hook
- yarn

USES

- accessories
- main body

STITCHES USED

- single crochet
- double crochet
- chain stitch

THE STITCH

Number of Stitches: multiples of 3
sts +1

Row 1: 1 ch to turn, *1 sc, 2 ch, skip 2
sts,* 1 sc

Row 2: 3 ch to turn, 1 dc, *3 dc in each
sc on the prev rw,* 2 dc in the last sc

Row 3: 1 ch to turn, 1 sc, *2 ch, 1 sc
inserted under the top stitch of the
2nd dc in each group,* 2 ch, 1 sc

After rows 1–3, keep repeating rows 2
and 3.

TECHNIQUE

1. Row 1 is a preparation. Make 1
chain stitch to turn, then keep
repeating: 1 single crochet, 2
chain stitches, skip 2 stitches.
Finish the row with 1 single
crochet.

2▼ For row 2, make 3 chain stitches
to turn, then 1 double crochet.
Then, make 3 double crochets
inserted into each single crochet
in the previous row. Finish with 2
double crochets in the last single
crochet.

3▲ For row 3, make 1 chain stitch to
turn, then 1 single crochet, and
then keep repeating: 2 chain
stitches and 1 single crochet
inserted under the top stitch of
the middle double crochet in
each group of 3 double crochet
stitches in the previous row.
Finish the row with 2 chain
stitches and a single crochet.

Tip

The little palms are formed by groups
of three vertical double crochets.

¤

Starry Stitch

The extended single crochet, made with two consecutive insertions, gives this stitch a slightly starry appearance.

EQUIPMENT

- crochet hook
- yarn

USES

- accessories
- main body

STITCHES USED

- extended single crochet
- single crochet
- chain stitch

THE STITCH

Number of Stitches: multiples of 4 sts +1

Row 1: 2 ch to turn, *insert hook, 1 yarn over, pull 1 loop, insert hook into the nxt st, 1 yarn over, pull 1 loop, 1 yarn over, draw through 3 loops, 1 ch,* 1 sc

Repeat this row as many times as needed.

VARIANT

Alternate inserting the hook under the front loop in one row and the back loop in the next.

Tip

For orientation, with each insertion, yarn over once and pull through a loop, then yarn over again and draw through 3 loops.

¤

TECHNIQUE

1▼ Make 2 chain stitches to turn, then repeat the following steps: Insert the hook under the top stitch, yarn over once, and pull 1 loop. You'll now have 2 loops on your hook.

2▲ Insert the hook under the next top stitch. Yarn over once and pull 1 loop. You'll be left with 3 stitches on your hook.

3. Do 1 final yarn over and thread the yarn through the 3 loops. Add 1 chain stitch. Finish the row with 1 single crochet.

Waffle Stitch

The distinctive relief in this design is created by an extended single crochet made with two insertions.

EQUIPMENT

- crochet hook
- yarn

USES

- accessories
- main body

STITCHES USED

- chain stitch
- extended single crochet

THE STITCH

Number of Stitches: pairs
Row 1: 2 ch to turn, *insert hook under the top stitch, 1 yarn over, pull 1 loop, insert hook in the nxt st, 1 yarn over, pull 1 loop, x2 (1 yarn over, draw through 2 loops), 1 ch*
Row 2: 2 ch to turn, *insert hook in front of the long st, 1 yarn over, pull 1 loop, insert hook under the nxt top st, 1 yarn over, pull 1 loop, x2 (1 yarn over, draw through 2 loops), 1 ch*
After rows 1 and 2, keep repeating row 2.

Tip

For orientation, after each insertion comes 1 yarn over and 1 pulled loop; then 1 yarn over and 2 loops drawn through done twice.

¤

TECHNIQUE

1. Row 1 is a preparation. Make 2 chain stitches to turn, then repeat the following steps: Insert the hook under the top stitch, yarn over once ▼ and pull 1 loop. You'll now have 2 loops on your hook.

2. ▲ Insert under next stitch, 1 yarn over, pull 1 loop, 1 yarn over, pull yarn through 2 loops.* Do 1 final yarn over and thread the yarn through the 2 loops.
3. All the rows that follow are identical to the first. However, the hook is inserted on either side of the lengthened stitch to form the extended single crochet.

Shell Stitch

Double crochets combined in a single stitch create a decorative design in the form of adjacent slats.

EQUIPMENT

- crochet hook
- yarn

USES

- borders
- accessories
- main body

STITCHES USED

- single crochet
- double crochet

THE STITCH

Number of Stitches: multiples of 5 sts +4

Row 1: 3 ch to turn, 3 dc in 1 st, skip 2 sts, 1 sc, *skip 2 sts, 5 dc in 1 st, skip 1 st, 1 sc*

Row 2: 3 ch to turn, 3 dc in the sc on the prev rw, *1 sc under the top st of the 3rd dc, 5 dc in the sc on the prev rw,* 1 sc

After rows 1 and 2, keep repeating row 2.

VARIANT

For smaller shells, use a stitch count of multiples of 4 sts +1.

Row 1: 1 ch to turn, *1 sc, skip 1 st, 3 dc in 1 st, skip 1 st,* 1 sc

Row 2: 3 ch to turn, 1 dc, *1 sc in the middle dc of the prev rw, 3 dc in the sc of the prev rw,* 2 dc

TECHNIQUE

1. Make 3 chain stitches to turn, then 3 double crochets in the same stitch, skip 2 stitches, and do 1 single crochet. Next, repeat the following steps to complete the row: Skip 2 stitches, make 5 double crochets in a single stitch, skip 1 stitch, make 1 single crochet.

2. For row 2, make 3 chain stitches to turn, then 3 double crochets in the single crochet on the previous row. Then repeat: 1 single crochet inserted under the top stitch of the 3rd double crochet in the previous row ▲, then 5 double crochets in the single crochet on the previous row ◄. Finish with 1 single crochet.

Tip

The single crochet is placed in the middle of the group of five double crochets, formed from the single crochet that separates them.

◻

Moss Stitch

Sometimes referred to as the "linen stitch" because of the comb-like arrangement of the stitches, this regular design is popular for its graphic quality.

EQUIPMENT

- crochet hook
- yarn

USES

- borders
- main body

STITCHES USED

- single crochet
- chain stitch

THE STITCH

Number of Stitches: pairs
Row 1: 1 ch to turn, *skip 1 st, in 1 same st (1 sc, 2 ch, 1 sc)*
Row 2: 1 ch to turn, *(1 sc, 2 ch, 1 sc) inserting under each ch in the prev rw*
After rows 1 and 2, keep repeating row 2.

TECHNIQUE

1. Row 1 is a preparation. Make 1 chain stitch to turn, and repeat the following steps to complete the row: Skip 1 stitch, then in the next stitch: Make 1 single crochet, 2 chain stitches, and 1 single crochet.

2. All the rows that follow are identical to the first. Make 1 chain stitch to turn and repeat the following steps to complete the row: Insert the hook under the 2 chain stitches in the previous row, ◄ then make 1 single crochet, 2 chain stitches ▲, and 1 single crochet.

Tip

For orientation, the chain stitches form a small arch over the little pillars created by the stitch.

¤

Back Cross Stitch

This stitch gets its name from the way the double crochet connects one stitch to the next.

EQUIPMENT

- crochet hook
- yarn

USES

- accessories
- main body

STITCHES USED

- double crochet
- chain stitch

THE STITCH

Number of Stitches: multiples of 3 sts +2

Row 1: 3 ch, 1 dc, *1 yarn over, insert hook into the prev st, 1 yarn over, pull 1 loop, skip 2 sts, 1 yarn over, insert hook, 1 yarn over, pull 1 loop, 1 yarn over, draw through 5 loops, 2 ch,* 1 dc

Row 2: 3 ch, 1 dc, *1 yarn over, insert hook into the prev st, 1 yarn over, pull 1 loop, skip 2 sts, 1 yarn over, insert hook into the st holding the 5 loops, 1 yarn over, pull 1 loop, 1 yarn over, draw through 5 loops, 2 ch,* 1 dc

After rows 1 and 2, keep repeating row 2.

Tip

For orientation, the stitch forms broken vertical lines created by overlapping the two insertions.

¤

TECHNIQUE

1. Row 1 is a preparation. Make 3 chain stitches to turn, then 1 double crochet, and then repeat: Yarn over once, insert the hook into the same stitch as the double crochet, yarn over again, pull 1 loop, skip 2 stitches, yarn over once more. You'll have 3 loops and 1 yarn over ▼.

2. Insert the hook into the next stitch and pull 1 loop, yarn over once, and pull yarn through the 5 loops.* Make 2 chain stitches. Finish the row with 1 double crochet.

3▲ All the rows that follow are almost identical to the first. Instead of skipping 2 stitches, insert the hook into the stitch that holds the 5 loops in the previous row.

Herringbone Stitch

Compact and striking, the herringbone stitch owes its slightly ribbed appearance to the lengthened stitches.

EQUIPMENT

- crochet hook
- yarn

USES

- accessories
- main body

STITCHES USED

- single crochet
- long stitch

THE STITCH

Number of Stitches: multiples of 2 sts
Row 1: 1 ch to turn, sc for the rest of the row
Row 2: 1 ch to turn, *1 lengthened st inserted under the sc in the prev rw, 1 sc*
After rows 1 and 2, keep repeating row 2.

Tip

Single crochets and lengthened stitches are alternated across two rows. This means that a single crochet becomes a lengthened stitch in the next row, and vice versa.

¤

TECHNIQUE

1. For row 1, make 1 chain stitch to turn, and then continue with single crochets for the rest of the row.

2 ▲ For row 2, make 1 chain stitch to turn, then repeat the following steps: Insert the hook under the single crochet in the previous row.

3. Yarn over once and pull 1 loop. This first loop is lengthened ▲. Yarn over once more and draw through 2 loops. Make 1 single crochet in the next stitch. Continue like this to the end of the row.

Mesh
Stitches

Mesh Stitch

The combination of chain stitches and double crochets forms an open grid.

EQUIPMENT

- crochet hook
- yarn

USES

- accessories
- main body

STITCHES USED

- chain stitch
- double crochet

THE STITCH

Number of Stitches: multiples of 3 sts +4

Row 1: 4 ch to turn, skip 3 sts, 1 dc, *2 ch, skip 2 sts, 1 dc*

Row 2: 4 ch to turn, skip 3 sts, *1 dc, 2 ch, skip 2 sts,* 1 dc

After rows 1 and 2, keep repeating row 2.

VARIANT

For a tighter mesh, especially when using fine yarn, work on a count of 2 sts +2

Row 1: 4 ch to turn, skip 1 st, 1 dc, *1 ch, skip 1 st, 1 dc*

Row 2: 4 ch to turn, skip 2 sts, *1 dc, 1 ch, skip 1 st,* 1 dc

TECHNIQUE

1. Row 1 is a preparation for the following rows. Make 4 chain stitches to turn. Make 1 double crochet in the 8th stitch away from the hook. Then repeat the following steps: Make 2 chain stitches ▾, insert the hook in the 3rd stitch along, and make 1 double crochet. Continue like this to the end of the row.

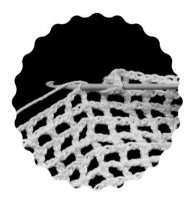

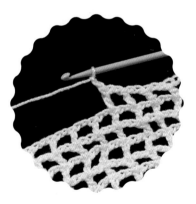

2. For row 2 onward, make 4 chain stitches to turn. The first double crochet is inserted under the top stitch of the first double crochet ▲ in the previous row. Make ◂ 2 chain stitches, then insert the hook into the next double crochet to make a new double crochet. Finish with 1 double crochet.

Tip

For orientation, the double crochets are aligned vertically and separated by two chain stitches.

¤

Offset Mesh Stitch

Attaching the double crochets to the chain stitches automatically offsets the grid squares.

EQUIPMENT

- crochet hook
- yarn

USES

- accessories
- main body

STITCHES USED

- chain stitch
- double crochet

THE STITCH

Number of Stitches: multiples of 2 sts +1

Row 1: 3 ch to turn, 1 dc, *1 ch, skip 1 st, 1 dc*

Row 2: 3 ch to turn, 1 dc under the ch in the prev rw, *1 ch, 1 dc under the ch in the prev rw*

After rows 1 and 2, keep repeating row 2.

VARIANT

For a looser mesh, work on a multiple of 4 sts +1.

Row 1: 5 ch to turn, 1 dc, *4 ch, skip 2 sts, 1 dc*

Row 2: 5 ch to turn, 1 dc under the ch in the prev rw, *4 ch, 1 dc under the ch in the prev rw*

After rows 1 and 2, keep repeating row 2.

TECHNIQUE

1. Make 3 chain stitches to turn. Insert the hook in the 4th stitch away from the hook, and make 1 double crochet. Then repeat the following steps to complete the row: 1 chain stitch, skip 2 stitches, make 1 double crochet in the next stitch.

2. For row 2 onward, make 3 chain stitches to turn, then 1 double crochet inserted under the chain stitches in the previous row. Then repeat: 1 chain stitch ◄ and 1 double crochet ▲ under each chain stitch in the previous row.

Tip

For orientation, all the double crochets are offset vertically and separated by a chain stitch.

¤

Lace Mesh Stitch

This netting is made up of double crochets uniformly supported at the bottom.

EQUIPMENT

- crochet hook
- yarn

USES

- main body

STITCHES USED

- single crochet
- double crochet
- chain stitch

THE STITCH

Number of Stitches: multiples of 4 sts +1

Row 1: 5 ch to turn, *1 dc, 3 ch, skip 3 sts,* 1 dc

Row 2: 2 ch to turn, *2 ch, 1 sc in the middle ch, 2 ch, 1 dc under the top st of the double crochet in the prev rw,* 2 ch, 1 sc

Row 3: 5 ch to turn, *1 dc under the top st of the double crochet in the prev rw, 3 ch,* 1 dc

After rows 1–3, keep repeating rows 2 and 3.

Tip

For orientation, double crochets are present in every row and always aligned vertically.

¤

TECHNIQUE

1. Row 1 is a preparation for the following rows. Make 5 chain stitches to turn and repeat the following: 1 double crochet, 3 chain stitches, and skip 3 stitches. Finish with 1 double crochet.

2. For row 2, make 2 chain stitches to turn and repeat: 2 chain stitches, 1 single crochet inserted into the middle of the chain stitches ▲ in the previous row, 2 chain stitches . . .

3.▲ . . . make 1 double crochet inserted under the top stitch of the double crochet in the previous row. Finish the row with 2 chain stitches and a single crochet in the selvage stitch.

4. For row 3, the double crochets are attached to the double crochets in the previous row and separated by 3 chain stitches.

Honeycomb Mesh Stitch

This airy stitch is made up of small bridges arranged in staggered rows and joined together with single crochets.

EQUIPMENT

- crochet hook
- yarn

USES

- accessories

STITCHES USED

- single crochet
- chain stitch

THE STITCH

Number of Stitches: multiples of 4 sts +4

Row 1: 5 ch to turn, skip 3 sts, 1 sc, *5 ch, skip 3 sts, 1 sc*

Row 2: 5 ch to turn, *1 sc in the middle st of the 5 ch in the prev rw, 5 ch,* 1 sc After rows 1 and 2, keep repeating row 2.

TECHNIQUE

1. Make 5 chain stitches to turn. Insert the hook into the 9th stitch away from the hook and make 1 single crochet.

2.▲ Make 5 chain stitches, skip 3 stitches in the foundation chain, and make 1 single crochet in the next stitch. Repeat to the end of the row.

3. For row 2 onward, make 5 chain stitches to turn.

4. Repeat: Insert the hook into the middle stitch of the 5 chain stitches in the previous row ▼ to form an arch, and make 1 single crochet. Make 5 chain stitches ◄. Finish with 1 single crochet at the end of the row.

Tip

For orientation, each arch should always be positioned across the middle of two arches in the previous row.

¤

Picot Lattice Stitch

This stitch is made using the same technique as for the honeycomb lattice stitch, with a decorative picot added at each junction.

EQUIPMENT

- crochet hook
- yarn

USES

- accessories

STITCHES USED

- single crochet
- slip stitch
- chain stitch

THE STITCH

Number of Stitches: multiples of 5 sts +7

Row 1: 5 ch, skip 2 sts, 1 sc, 3 ch, 1 sl st in the prev sc, *5 ch, skip 3 sts, 1 sc, 3 ch, 1 sl st in the prev sc,* 5 ch, skip 3 sts, 1 sc

Row 2: *5 ch, 1 sc inserted under the middle of the arch, 3 ch, 1 sl st in the prev sc,* 5 ch, 1 sc

After rows 1 and 2, keep repeating row 2.

Tip

The picots are always attached to the middle of an arch and are made up of a single crochet, 3 chain stitches, and a slip stitch.

¤

TECHNIQUE

1. Row 1 is a preparation. Make 5 chain stitches to turn, and insert the hook into the 8th stitch away from the hook. To create the first picot, make 1 single crochet, 3 chain stitches, and 1 slip stitch inserted into the previous single crochet.

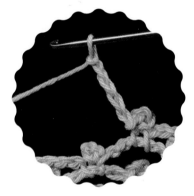

Repeat: 5 chain stitches ▲, skip 3 stitches, and make 1 picot. Finish with 1 single crochet.

2. For the subsequent rows, repeat the following steps: 5 chain stitches ◄, 1 single crochet inserted under the middle of each arch, 3 chain stitches, and 1 slip stitch inserted into the previous single crochet ▲. Finish the row with 5 chain stitches and a single crochet in the last stitch in the row.

Picot Mesh Stitch

This mesh is made up of small hexagons, with a picot on one side.

EQUIPMENT

- crochet hook
- yarn

USES

- accessories

STITCHES USED

- slip stitch
- double crochet
- chain stitch

THE STITCH

Number of Stitches: multiples of 5 sts +3

Row 1: 3 ch to turn, 7 ch, 1 sl st in the 4ᵗʰ prev ch, 2 ch, skip 2 sts in the foundation chain, 1 dc, *7 ch, 1 sl st in the 4ᵗʰ prev ch, 2 ch, skip 4 sts in the foundation chain, 1 dc*

Row 2: 3 ch to turn, *7 ch, 1 sl st in the 4ᵗʰ prev ch, 2 ch, 1 dc in the 2ⁿᵈ ch after the picot in the prev rw*

After rows 1 and 2, keep repeating row 2.

Tip

For neater, more even work, tighten the slip stitch to close the picot.

¤

TECHNIQUE

1. Row 1 is a preparation for the following rows. Place a marker on the last stitch in the foundation chain. Make 3 chain stitches to turn. Add 7 chain stitches, and make 1 slip stitch in the 4ᵗʰ one to create a picot ▼. Add 2 chain stitches, skip 2 stitches in the foundation chain (insert 2 stitches before the marker), and make 1 double crochet.

2. Complete the row by repeating the steps from the 7 chain stitches, skipping 4 stitches before the double crochet.

3▲ The steps are the same for the rest of the rows. The double crochet is formed by inserting the hook into the 2ⁿᵈ stitch after the picot in the previous row.

Picot Trellis Stitch

This elegant stitch lines up the picots by crossing the double crochets.

EQUIPMENT

- crochet hook
- yarn

USES

- accessories
- borders
- main body

STITCHES USED

- single crochet
- double crochet
- chain stitch

THE STITCH

Number of Stitches: multiples of 4 sts +1

Row 1: 3 ch to turn, *1 sc, 3 ch, 1 sc in the prev sc, 1 sc, 2 ch, skip 2 sts,* 1 sc

Row 2: 3 ch to turn, *1 dc inserted under the 2 ch in the prev rw, 3 ch, 1 sc in the prev dc, 1 dc inserted under the same 2 ch in the prev rw, 2 ch,* 1 dc inserted under the 3 ch in the prev rw After rows 1 and 2, keep repeating row 2.

Tip

For orientation, the two chain stitches form bridges to which the picots are attached.

¤

TECHNIQUE

1. Make 3 chain stitches to turn and repeat the following: 1 single crochet, 3 chain stitches, 1 single crochet inserted into the stitch just made to close the picot, 1 single crochet, 2 chain stitches, skip 2 stitches. Finish the row with 1 single crochet.

2. For the rest of the rows, make 3 chain stitches to turn and repeat the following steps: Insert the hook under the 2 chain stitches in the previous row and make 1 double crochet ▲, 3 chain stitches, 1 single crochet in the double crochet just made ◄, 1 double crochet inserted under the same 2 chain stitches in the previous row, and 2 chain stitches. Finish the row with 1 double crochet attached to the 3 chain stitches in the previous row.

Ladder Stitch

Also known as the "string network stitch," this design creates a ladder-like pattern by combining chain stitches.

EQUIPMENT

- crochet hook
- yarn

USES

- accessories

STITCHES USED

- single crochet
- double crochet
- chain stitch

THE STITCH

Number of Stitches: multiples of 7 sts +4

Row 1: 1 ch to turn, *5 ch, skip 5 sts, 1 sc, 3 ch, 1 sc,* 5 ch, skip 5 sts, 1 dc
Row 2: 1 ch to turn, *5 ch, (1 sc, 3 ch, 1 sc) in the arch made by 3 ch in the prev rw,* 5 ch, 1 dc in the selvage sts
After rows 1 and 2, keep repeating row 2.

Tip

The ladders should be aligned. For orientation, the group made up of single crochets and three chain stitches forms the link between the bars of five chain stitches.

¤

TECHNIQUE

1. Row 1 is a preparation for the following rows. Make a chain stitch to turn, then repeat the following steps: 5 chain stitches ▼, skip 5 stitches, 1 single crochet,

3 chain stitches, and 1 single crochet in the next stitch. Finish with 5 chain stitches, skip 5 stitches, and a double crochet in the last stitch in the row.

2. For the following rows, make 1 chain stitch to turn and repeat the following steps: 5 chain stitches ◄, insert the hook under the 3 chain stitches in the prev row ▲, and make 1 single crochet, 3 chain stitches, and 1 single crochet. Finish the row with 2 chain stitches and a double crochet inserted under the selvage stitches.

Open Stitches

Iris Stitch

Tiny shells seem to take root on branches formed by double crochets.

EQUIPMENT

- crochet hook
- yarn

USES

- accessories
- main body

STITCHES USED

- single crochet
- double crochet
- chain stitch

THE STITCH

Number of Stitches: multiples of 6 sts +3

Row 1: 1 ch, 1 sc, *1 ch, 3 sc, 2 ch, 3 sc,* 2 sc

Row 2: 3 ch, 1 sc, *(2 dc, 1 ch, 2 dc) under the 2 ch in the prev rw, (1 dc, 2 ch, 1 dc) under the ch in the prev rw,* 1 dc under the ch

Complete rows 1 and 2, then keep repeating row 2.

TECHNIQUE

1. Row 1 is a preparation. Make 1 chain stitch to turn and 1 single crochet. Then repeat: 1 chain stitch, 3 single crochets, 2 chain stitches, and 3 single crochets without skipping stitches.

2▼ In the rest of the rows, the first group of double crochets is inserted under the 2 chain stitches in the previous row. Make 2 double crochets, 1 chain stitch, and 2 double crochets.

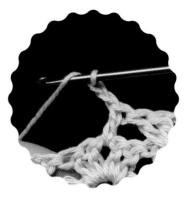

3. Under the chain stitch in the previous row, make the second group of double crochets: 1 double crochet, 2 chain stitches ▲, and 1 double crochet.

Tip

For orientation, rows alternate between shells made of two and four double crochets. These are always formed above a group of two double crochets.

¤

Wicker Stitch

The overlapping of the double crochets resembles the spiral coils found on certain shellfish.

EQUIPMENT

- crochet hook
- yarn

USES

- borders
- main body

STITCHES USED

- chain stitch
- double crochet

THE STITCH

Number of Stitches: multiples of 3 sts
Row 1: 2 ch to turn, *1 dc, 1 ch, 1 dc, skip 1 st*
Row 2: 2 ch to turn, *(1 dc, 1 ch, 1 dc) under each ch*
After rows 1 and 2, keep repeating row 2.

VARIANT

To stagger the stitch, alternate rows with double crochets inserted under the chain stitches, and rows with double crochets inserted between the chain stitches in the previous row.

Tip

For orientation, the two new double crochets in row 2 are placed in the middle of the V, formed by the two double crochets that are separate from the chain stitch in the previous row.

¤

TECHNIQUE

1. Row 1 is a preparation. Make 2 chain stitches to turn, then repeat the following steps to complete the row: 1 double crochet, 1 chain stitch, and skip 1 stitch.

2. For row 2 onward, make 2 chain stitches to turn. Repeat: under the chain stitches in the previous row, make 1 double crochet ▲, a chain stitch ◄, and then another double crochet ▼.

Checkerboard Stitch

With its even squares that alternate between solid and open, this stitch reproduces a fabric checkered pattern.

EQUIPMENT

- crochet hook
- yarn

USES

- accessories

STITCHES USED

- chain stitch
- double crochet

THE STITCH

Number of Stitches: multiples of 6 sts +6

Row 1: 2 ch to turn, 2 dc, *3 ch, skip 3 sts, 3 dc,* 3 ch, skip 3 sts, 1 dc

Row 2: 2 ch to turn, 2 dc under the 3 ch in the prev rw, *3 ch, 3 dc under the 3 ch in the prev rw,* 3 ch, 1 dc under the selvage sts

After rows 1 and 2, keep repeating row 2.

TECHNIQUE

1. Row 1 is a preparation for the following rows. Make 2 chain stitches to turn and 2 double crochets, then repeat the following steps: 3 chain stitches, skip 3 stitches, 3 double crochets to complete the row. Finish with 3 chain stitches, skip 3 stitches, and a double crochet.

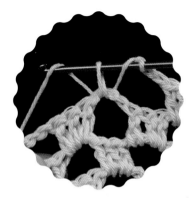

2. For row 2 onward, make 2 chain stitches to turn. Insert the hook under the 3 chain stitches in the previous row and make 2 double crochets. Then repeat the following under each group of 3 chain stitches: 3 chain stitches ◄ and 3 double crochets ▲. Finish the row with 3 chain stitches and a double crochet in the selvage stitches.

Tip

For orientation, the groups of three double crochets are not aligned with those in the previous row and are always attached to the chain stitches in the previous row.

¤

Open Arches Stitch

A series of double crochets attached to arches form small, uniform squares.

EQUIPMENT

- crochet hook
- yarn

USES

- accessories
- main body

STITCHES USED

- single crochet
- double crochet
- chain stitch

THE STITCH

Number of Stitches: multiples of 5 sts +2

Row 1: 3 ch to turn, 1 dc, *4 dc, 1 ch, skip 1 st,* 1 dc

Row 2: 1 ch to turn, 1 sc, *4 ch, 1 sc inserted under the ch in the prev rw,* 1 sc

Row 3: 3 ch to turn, 1 dc, *4 dc inserted under each group of ch in the prev rw, 1 ch,* 1 dc

After rows 1–3, keep repeating rows 2 and 3.

VARIANT

For larger squares, replace the double crochets with treble crochets. For rows 1 and 3, make 5 chain stitches to turn.

TECHNIQUE

1. Row 1 is a preparation. Add 3 chain stitches to the foundation chain and make 1 double crochet in the 4th stitch away from the hook. Then repeat: 4 double crochets and 1 chain stitch, skip 1 stitch. Finish the row with 1 double crochet.

2▼ For row 2, the arches are made up of 4 chain stitches and are attached to the chain stitch in the previous row by a single crochet.

3◀ In row 3, the groups of 4 double crochets are attached to the arches in the previous row and separated by a chain stitch.

Tip

For orientation, the tiles should always be aligned vertically.

¤

Scalloped Diamond Stitch

A lattice of diamond-shaped arches sets off a scallop of double crochets.

EQUIPMENT

- crochet hook
- yarn

USES

- accessories
- main body

STITCHES USED

- single crochet
- double crochet
- chain stitch

THE STITCH

Number of Stitches: multiples of 8 sts +1

Row 1: 1 ch to turn, *1 sc, 4 ch, skip 3 sts,* 1 sc

Row 2: 3 ch to turn, *4 dc under the ch in the prev rw, 2 ch, 1 sc under the following ch, 2 ch,* 1 dc

Row 3: 1 ch to turn, *1 sc under the ch, 4 ch, 1 sc before the 4 dc in the prev rw, 4 ch,* 1 sc

Row 4: 3 ch to turn, *2 ch, 1 sc under the arch, 2 ch, 4 dc under the nxt arch,* 1 dc

Row 5: 1 ch to turn, *4 ch, 1 sc before the dc, 4 ch, 1 sc under the nxt arch,* 1 sc

After these 5 rows, keep repeating rows 2–5.

TECHNIQUE

1▼ Rows 2 and 4 form the scallops. The 4 double crochets are made by inserting the hook under the chain stitches (arch) in the previous row. These groups of double crochets are separated by 2 chain stitches and 1 single crochet inserted under the next arch.

2▲ Rows 3 and 5 form the arches to which the double and single crochets in the next row will be attached. The single crochets are inserted before and after the group of 4 double crochets in the previous row.

Tip

For orientation, the groups of four double crochets are always offset and separated by a crosspiece.

¤

Triangle Stitch

This stitch is made up of small triangles arranged head-to-tail, whose apexes are angled according to the spacing of the double crochets.

EQUIPMENT

- crochet hook
- yarn

USES

- accessories
- main body

STITCHES USED

- chain stitch
- double crochet

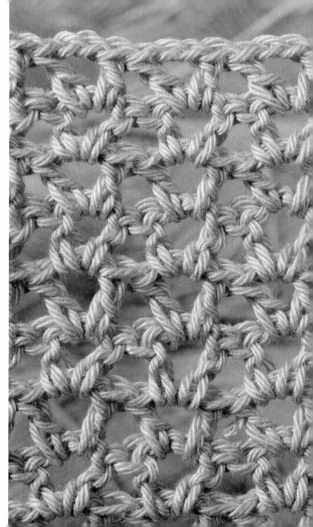

THE STITCH

Number of Stitches: multiples of 3 sts +1

Row 1: 5 ch to turn, 1 dc, *skip 2 sts, (1 dc, 2 ch, 1 dc) in the nxt st*

Row 2: 5 ch to turn, 1 dc inserted under the 2 ch in the prev rw, *(1 dc, 2 ch, 1 dc) inserted under the nxt 2 ch,* (1 dc, 2 ch, 1 dc) inserted under the 5 selvage ch

After rows 1 and 2, keep repeating row 2.

TECHNIQUE

1. Row 1 is a preparation for the following rows. Add 5 chain stitches to turn, and make 1 double crochet inserted into the 6ᵗʰ stitch away from the hook. Then repeat the following steps: Every 3 stitches, make 1 double crochet, 2 chain stitches, and 1 double crochet in the same stitch.

2. For row 2 onward, make 5 chain stitches to turn, then 1 double crochet inserted under the 2 chain stitches in the previous row. Then, under the next 2 chain stitches, repeat the group: 1 double crochet ◄, 2 chain stitches ▲, and 1 double crochet. The last group is made by inserting the hook under the selvage stitches.

Tip

For orientation, the double crochets in the previous row are either attached or separated by two chain stitches. In the next row, this space is the base of the group made up of one double crochet, two chain stitches, and one double crochet.

¤

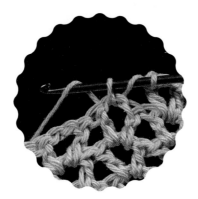

Rug Stitch

By crossing half double crochets, this stitch imitates the patterns on little bedside rugs.

EQUIPMENT

- crochet hook
- yarn

USES

- borders
- accessories
- main body

STITCHES USED

- Albanian stitch
- half double crochet

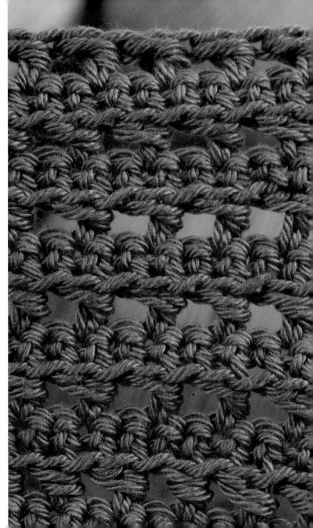

THE STITCH

Number of Stitches: multiples of 2 sts +3

Row 1: 1 ch to turn, 1 hdc, *skip 1 st, 1 hdc, 1 hdc inserted behind the prev hdc,* skip 1 st, 1 hdc

Row 2: 1 ch to turn, the rest of the rw in Albanian st, inserted under the front loop.

Repeat these two rows as many times as needed. This row represents the right side of the piece.

Tip

For orientation, the double crochets are not offset but must be vertically aligned.

¤

TECHNIQUE

1. Make 1 chain stitch to turn and 1 half double crochet. Repeat the following steps: Skip 1 stitch, make 1 half double crochet inserted into the next stitch.

2▼ To make the next half double crochet, yarn over once, and hook the previous double crochet from behind, and then repeat. Finish the row with a skipped stitch and 1 half double crochet.

3▲ For the next row, make a chain stitch to turn and then single crochets inserted under the front loop of the top stitch. The other loop, left loose, then forms a line across the piece.

Fan Stitch

Sets of treble crochets in the same stitch unfurl like fans.

EQUIPMENT

- crochet hook
- yarn

USES

- accessories

STITCHES USED

- single crochet
- chain stitch
- treble crochet

THE STITCH

Number of Stitches: multiples of 14 sts +1

Row 1: 1 ch to turn, 1 sc, *skip 6 sts, 13 tr in 1 st, skip 6 sts, 1 sc*

Row 2: 4 ch to turn, 1 tr, *5 ch, 1 sc in the 7th tr, 5 ch, 2 tr in the sc*

Row 3: 1 ch to turn, *1 sc between 2 tr, 13 tr in 1 sc,* 1 sc under the selvage sts

After rows 1–3, keep repeating rows 2 and 3.

Tip

For orientation, the chain stitches loop around the treble crochets and are separated by a single crochet, which will become the base for the set of treble crochets in the next row.

¤

TECHNIQUE

1. Row 1 is a preparation. Make 1 chain stitch to turn and 1 single crochet. Then repeat: Skip 6 stitches, make 13 treble crochets in the same stitch, skip 6 stitches, then make 1 single crochet.

2. For row 2, make 4 chain stitches to turn, then 1 treble crochet. Then repeat the following steps: 5 chain stitches, 1 single crochet in the 7th treble crochet in the previous row ▲, 5 chain stitches, and 2 treble crochets in the next single crochet stitch in the previous row.

3. For row 3, make 2 chain stitches to turn and repeat: 1 single crochet with the hook inserted between the 2 treble crochet in the previous row, and 13 treble crochets in the single crochet in the previous row ▲. Finish the row with 1 single crochet, inserting the hook under the selvage stitches.

Slanting Knotted Stitch

This simple, striking stitch is made up of a succession of knotted double crochets pointing left and right.

EQUIPMENT

- crochet hook
- yarn

USES

- accessories
- borders
- main body

STITCH USED

- double crochet

THE STITCH

Number of Stitches: any
Row 1: 2 ch to turn, 1 dc, *skip 1 st, 1 dc, 1 dc inserted behind the prev dc,* 1 dc Repeat this row as many times as needed.

VARIANT

For a more elongated stitch, replace the double crochets with treble or even double treble crochets. In the first case, make 4 chain stitches to turn, and for the second, 5 chain stitches.

TECHNIQUE

1▼ Make 2 chain stitches to turn and 1 double crochet, then repeat the following steps: Skip 1 stitch, make 1 double crochet, . . .

2▲ . . . and then another double crochet with the hook inserted around the back of the previous double crochet, rather than in the next stitch. Finish the row with 1 double crochet.

Tip

For orientation, the double crochets are vertically aligned. The second double crochet is attached alternately, depending on the row, to the right or left of the preceding double crochet.

Open Crown Stitch

A series of double crochets separated by chain stitches creates airy crowns.

EQUIPMENT

- crochet hook
- yarn

USES

- borders
- accessories

STITCHES USED

- chain stitch
- double crochet

THE STITCH

Number of Stitches: multiples of 4 sts +2

Row 1: 3 ch to turn, 1 dc, *skip 3 sts, in 1 same st (1 dc, 1 ch) x3 and 1 dc,* 1 dc

Row 2: ch to turn, 1 dc, *under the middle ch (1 dc, 1 ch) x3 and 1 dc,* 1 dc

After rows 1 and 2, keep repeating row 2.

Tip

For orientation, the motifs made up of four double crochets and three chain stitches are vertically aligned.

¤

TECHNIQUE

1. Row 1 is a preparation for the following rows. Make 3 chain stitches to turn and 1 double crochet, then repeat the following steps: Skip 3 stitches, then in the next stitch, repeat 3 times (1 double crochet and 1 chain stitch), add 1 double crochet in the same stitch. Finish the row with 1 double crochet.

2. All the rows that follow are identical to the first. Instead of skipping 3 stitches, insert the hook under the middle chain stitch in the group of 4 double crochets in the previous row ◄, then repeat 3 times (1 double crochet, 1 chain stitch) ▲, then 1 double crochet. Finish the row with 1 double crochet.

Ribbon Stitch

This stitch owes its name to the series of double crochets that create its distinctive ridges.

EQUIPMENT

- crochet hook
- yarn

USES

- accessories
- main body

STITCHES USED

- chain stitch
- double crochet

THE STITCH

Number of Stitches: multiples of 10 sts +3

Row 1: 3 ch to turn, 3 dc, *skip 3 sts, in 1 same st (2 dc, 2 ch, 2 dc), skip 3 sts, 3 dc*

Row 2: 3 ch to turn, 3 dc, *under the 2 ch in the prev rw (2 dc, 2 ch, 2 dc), 1 dc on each of the 3 dc in the prev rw* After rows 1 and 2, keep repeating row 2.

TECHNIQUE

1. Row 1 is a preparation for the following rows. Make 3 chain stitches to turn and 3 double crochets, then repeat the following steps: Skip 3 stitches, make 2 double crochets in the next stitch, 2 chain stitches, and 2 double crochets, then skip 3 stitches again and make 3 double crochets.

2. All the rows that follow are identical to the first. Instead of skipping 3 stitches, insert the hook under the 2 chain stitches in the previous row to make a group of 2 double crochets, then 2 chain stitches and 2 double crochets ▲. The next 3 double crochets are made by inserting the hook under the top stitch ◄ of each double crochet in the previous row.

Tip

For orientation, both the double crochets and the shells are vertically aligned.

¤

Flower Basket Lace Stitch

This decorative stitch features a basket of double crochets topped by chain stitch handle.

EQUIPMENT

- crochet hook
- yarn

USES

- accessories
- main body

STITCHES USED

- chain stitch
- single crochet
- double crochet
- treble crochet
- double treble crochet

ESSENTIAL CROCHET DICTIONARY

THE STITCH

Number of Stitches: multiples of 8 sts +1

Row 1: 1 ch to turn, *1 sc, 3 ch, skip 3 sts, in 1 st (1 dc, 3 ch, 1 dc), 3 ch, skip 3 sts,* 1 sc

Row 2: 5 ch to turn, *between each dc in the prev rw (3 tr, 2 ch, 3 tr),* 1 dtr in the selvage sts

Row 3: 3 ch to turn, *between each tr in the prev rw (1 dc, 3 ch, 1 dc), 3 ch, 1 sc in the junction, 3 ch,* 1 sc in the selvage sts

After rows 1–3, keep repeating rows 2 and 3.

Tip

For orientation, the double crochet starts with one yarn over, the treble crochet with two yarn overs, and the double treble crochet with three yarn overs.

¤

TECHNIQUE

1. Row 1 is a preparation. Make 1 chain stitch to turn and repeat the following steps: 1 single crochet, 3 chain stitches, skip 3 stitches, then in one same stitch (1 double crochet, 3 chain stitches, and 1 more double crochet), add 3 chain stitches, and skip 3 stitches.

2▲ For row 2, make 5 chain stitches to turn and repeat between each double crochet in the previous row. Then 3 treble crochets, 2 chain stitches, and 3 treble crochets. Finish the row with a double treble crochet in the selvage stitches.

3◄ Row 3 is identical to the first, but instead of skipping 3 stitches, insert the hook under the chain stitches that separate the groups of 3 double crochets in the previous row.

Open Cross Stitch

A treble crochet made on two stitches, then reinserted, creates the four prongs of a cross.

EQUIPMENT

- crochet hook
- yarn

USES

- borders
- accessories

STITCHES USED

- chain stitch
- single crochet
- double crochet
- treble crochet

THE STITCH

Number of Stitches: multiples of 3 sts +1

Row 1: 1 ch to turn, sc for the rest of the row

Row 2: 4 ch to turn, *2 yarn overs, insert the hook, pull 1 loop, 1 yarn over, draw through 2 loops, skip 1 st, 1 yarn over, insert the hook, pull 1 loop, x4 (1 yarn over, draw through 2 loops), 1 ch, 1 dc inserted between the 2 dc,* 1 tr

Repeat these two rows as many times as needed.

TECHNIQUE

1. For row 1, make 1 chain stitch to turn and then continue with single crochets for the rest of the row.
2. For row 2, make 4 chain stitches to turn, then repeat the following steps: 2 yarn overs, insert the hook under the top stitch, 1 yarn

over, pull 1 loop, 1 yarn over, pass the yarn through 2 loops. You'll be left with 3 stitches on your hook ▼.

3. Skip 1 stitch and yarn over once. Insert the hook under the next top stitch, yarn over, and pull 1 loop. Then repeat 4 times: 1 yarn over, pull the yarn through 2 loops. You'll be left with 1 stitch on your hook.

4. Make 1 chain stitch, 1 yarn over, insert the hook between the 2 prongs of the cross ▲, 1 yarn over, pull 1 loop, 1 yarn over, pull 2 loops, 1 yarn over, pass the yarn through the last 2 loops.

Tip

The crosses are vertically aligned. Don't forget to make a chain stitch before making the final double crochet in the cross.

¤

Lacy Rib Stitch

Two motifs made up of double crochets give a slightly ribbed look to the design.

EQUIPMENT

- crochet hook
- yarn

USES

- main body

STITCHES USED

- chain stitch
- double crochet

THE STITCH

Number of Stitches: multiples of 6 sts +2

Row 1: 3 ch to turn, *in 1 same st (2 dc, 1 ch, 2 dc), skip 2 sts, in 1 same st (1 dc, 1 ch, 1 dc), skip 2 sts,* in 1 same st (2 dc, 1 ch, 2 dc), 1 dc

Row 2: 3 ch to turn, *under the ch (2 dc, 1 ch, 2 dc), under the nxt ch (1 dc, 1 ch, 1 dc),* 1 dc

After rows 1 and 2, keep repeating row 2.

Tip

For orientation, the ribs are vertically aligned, so that each group of double crochets overlaps.

¤

TECHNIQUE

1. Row 1 is a preparation. Make 3 chain stitches to turn, then repeat the following steps: Insert the hook under the top stitch ▼ then make (2 double crochets, 1 chain stitch, and 2 double crochets).

2. Skip 2 stitches, then in the next stitch, make 1 double crochet, 1 chain stitch, and 1 double crochet. Skip 2 stitches. Finish with 2 double crochets, 1 chain stitch, and 2 double crochets in the same stitch, then 1 further double crochet.

3. For the rest of the rows, make 3 chain stitches to turn, then under each chain stitch in the previous row, alternate (2 double crochets, 1 chain stitch, 2 double crochets) ▲, and (1 double crochet, 1 chain stitch, 1 double crochet). Finish the row with 1 double crochet.

English Lace Stitch

Reminiscent of broderie anglaise, *this stitch forms arches in which sets of double crochets are joined together.*

EQUIPMENT
- crochet hook
- yarn

USES
- accessories
- borders

STITCHES USED
- single crochet
- double crochet
- chain stitch

THE STITCH

Number of Stitches: multiples of 3 sts +4

Row 1: 3 ch to turn, dc for the rest of the rw

Row 2: 4 ch to turn, *3 dc keeping 1 st on the hoot, 1 yarn over, draw through 4 sts, 4 ch,* 3 dc keeping 1 st on the hook, 1 yarn over, draw through 4 sts, 2 ch, 1 dc

Row 3: 3 ch to turn, 1 sc, *4 ch, 1 sc under each group of ch,* 2 ch, 1 sc

Row 4: like row 2, inserting the hook under each group of ch

Row 5: 3 ch to turn, 1 dc inserted under the ch, *3 dc inserted under each group of ch,* 1 sc under the selvage sts

After rows 1–5, keep repeating rows 2–5.

TECHNIQUE

1. For rows 2 and 4, make 4 chain stitches to turn, then repeat: 3 double crochets without drawing through the last stitch. You'll be left with 4 stitches on your hook, yarn over once ▼, and pass the yarn through all 4 stitches, then make 4 chain stitches. Finish the row with 2 chain stitches and a double crochet.

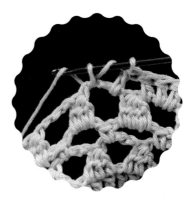

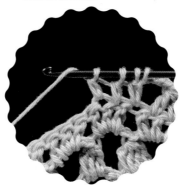

2. In row 3, the arches of 4 chain stitches are placed to support the double crochets in row 4.

3.▲ In row 5, make 3 chain stitches to turn, then 1 double crochet inserted under the chain stitches in the previous row. Then make 3 double crochets under each group of chain stitches. Finish the row with 1 single crochet.

Tip

This five-row stitch can be used as a yoke or border.

¤

Lacy Basket Stitch

The interweaving of double and single crochets is reminiscent of plant-fiber weaving.

EQUIPMENT

- crochet hook
- yarn

USES

- borders
- main body
- accessories

STITCHES USED

- single crochet
- double crochet
- chain stitch

ESSENTIAL CROCHET DICTIONARY

THE STITCH

Number of Stitches: multiples of 3 sts +2

Row 1: 3 ch to turn, in 1 st (1 dc, 2 ch, 1 sc), *skip 2 sts, in 1 st (2 dc, 2 ch, 1 sc),* 1 dc

Row 2: 3 ch to turn, 1 dc, *under each group of 2 ch (2 dc, 2 ch, 1 sc),* 1 dc in the selvage sts

After rows 1 and 2, keep repeating row 2.

Tip

For orientation, from row 2 onward, the chain stitches form a small arch over each group of stitches. In the next row, these arches become the base for groups of stitches.

¤

TECHNIQUE

1. Row 1 is a preparation. Make 3 chain stitches to turn, and in the next stitch: 1 double crochet, 2 chain stitches, and 1 single crochet. Then repeat the following steps for the rest of the row: Skip 2 stitches, in the next stitch (1 double crochet, 2 chain stitches, and 1 single crochet) ▼. Finish the row with 1 double crochet in the last stitch.

2▲ For row 2 onward, make 3 chain stitches to turn, then 1 double crochet. Then repeat under each group of chain stitches in the previous row (1 double crochet, 2 chain stitches, and 1 single crochet). Finish the row with 1 double crochet inserted under the selvage chain stitches.

Relief
Stitches

Puff Stitch

Several double crochets are drawn through together to create puffy little balls.

EQUIPMENT
- crochet hook
- yarn

USES
- borders
- main body

STITCHES USED
- double crochet
- chain stitch

THE STITCH

Number of Stitches: pairs

Row 1: 3 ch to turn, *x3 in the same st (1 yarn over, insert hook in 1 st, 1 yarn over, pull 1 loop, 1 yarn over, pull through 2 loops), 1 yarn over, draw through the 4 sts, 1 ch, skip 1 st*

Row 2: 3 ch to turn, *x3 in each ch in the prev rw (1 yarn over, insert hook in 1 st, 1 yarn over, pull 1 loop, 1 yarn over, pull through 2 loops), 1 yarn over, draw through the 4 sts, 1 ch, skip 1 st* After rows 1 and 2, keep repeating row 2.

VARIANT

The row of puff balls can be separated by a row of single or double crochets.

TECHNIQUE

1. The puff balls in row 1 are formed by repeating the same stitch 3 times: 1 yarn over, insert hook under the top stitch, 1 yarn over, pass the yarn through the top stitch, 1 yarn over, pull the yarn through 2 stitches. At this stage, you'll be left with 4 stitches on your hook ▼.

2. Yarn over and pull the yarn through the 4 stitches. Make 1 chain stitch and skip 1 stitch to make the next puff ball.

3.▲ From row 2 onward, insert the hook under the chain stitch in the previous row to make each puff ball.

Tip

For orientation, the puff balls are separated by one stitch in the same row and offset from one row to the next, since they are formed from the chain stitch in the previous row.

¤

Relief Double Crochet Stitch

By inserting the hook into the double crochets in the previous row, the top stitches are released, creating a raised line on the right side.

EQUIPMENT

- crochet hook
- yarn

USES

- accessories
- borders

STITCHES USED

- double crochet
- extended double crochet

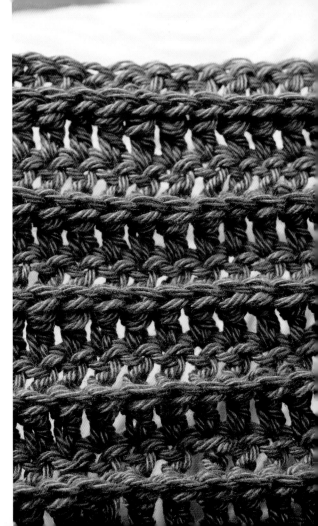

THE STITCH

Number of Stitches: any
Row 1: 2 ch to turn, the rest in dc
Row 2: 2 ch to turn, the rest in extended dc inserted in front
Repeat these two rows as many times as needed. Row 2 is the right side.

VARIANT

For a tighter pattern, complete rows 1 and 2, then make extended double crochets inserted behind the rest of the odd rows.

TECHNIQUE

1▼ In row 1, make 2 chain stitches to turn, then 1 double crochet in each stitch in the row.

2▲ For row 2, start with 2 chain stitches to turn. Then make 1 row of extended double crochets, inserting the hook in front around the double crochet in the previous row.

Tip

To make extended double crochets, the hook goes around the double crochet in the previous row without attaching to the stitches.

¤

Pineapple Stitch

Based on the puff stitch, the pineapple stitch is made up of a large number of stitches drawn together.

EQUIPMENT

- crochet hook
- yarn

USES

- borders
- accessories

STITCHES USED

- double crochet
- chain stitch

THE STITCH

Number of Stitches: pairs

Row 1: 2 ch to turn, *x4 in 1 same st (1 yarn over, insert hook under 1 st, 1 yarn over, pull 1 loop), 1 yarn over, draw through 8 sts, 1 yarn over, draw through 2 sts, 1 ch, skip 1 st*

Row 2: 2 ch to turn, *x4 in 1 same st (1 yarn over, insert hook under the ch in the prev rw, 1 yarn over, pull 1 loop), 1 yarn over, draw through 8 sts, 1 yarn over, draw through 2 sts, 1 ch, skip 1 st*

After rows 1 and 2, keep repeating row 2.

Tip

Avoid tightening the stitches created by the yarn overs, or the yarn overs themselves, to allow the hook to pass through them more easily when forming a puff ball.

✄

TECHNIQUE

1▼ For row 1, make 2 chain stitches to turn and repeat the following steps 4 times: Yarn over once, insert the hook under a stitch, yarn over again, and pull 1 loop. You'll be left with 9 stitches on your hook.

2► Continue with 1 yarn over and pull the yarn through 8 stitches. Yarn over 1 last time and pull the yarn through 2 stitches to seal the puff ball. Make 1 chain stitch and skip 1 stitch.

3▲ Row 2 is identical to row 1, except that the hook is inserted under the chain stitch in the previous row.

Bobble Bridge Stitch

Set along open lines, the little bobbles are puff balls separated by double crochet arches.

EQUIPMENT

- crochet hook
- yarn

USES

- borders
- accessories

STITCHES USED

- half double crochet
- double treble crochet

THE STITCH

Number of Stitches: multiples of 4 sts +1

Row 1: 2 ch to turn, the rest in hdc
Row 2: 2 ch to turn, 1 hdc, *3 ch, skip 3 sts, 1 hdc*
Row 3: 2 ch to turn, 1 hdc, *3 hdc under the ch, 3 dtr under the hdc without drawing through the last st, 1 yarn over, draw through 4 loops,* 3 hdc under the ch, 1 hdc in the last st
After rows 1–3, keep repeating rows 2 and 3.

Tip

In the next two rows, the half double crochet is made on the stitch that connects the three double treble crochets.

¤

TECHNIQUE

1. Row 1 is a preparation. Make 2 chain stitches to turn, then continue with half double crochets.
2. For row 2, make 2 chain stitches to turn, then 1 half double crochet. Then repeat: 3 chain stitches, skip 3 stitches, and 1 half double crochet.

3. For row 3, make 2 chain stitches to turn, then 1 half double crochet. Then repeat: 3 half double crochets inserted under the chain stitches ◄, and 3 double treble crochets inserted under the top stitch of the half double crochet in the previous row. Don't draw through the last loop. You'll have 4 loops on the hook ▲. Yarn over once and draw through the 4 loops.
4. Finish the row with 3 half double crochets under the chain stitches and 1 double crochet inserted under the last top stitch.

Double Crochet Rib Stitch

The extended stitch creates a ribbed look, reminiscent of knitting.

EQUIPMENT

- crochet hook
- yarn

USES

- accessories
- borders
- main body

STITCHES USED

- single crochet
- double crochet
- extended double crochet

THE STITCH

Number of Stitches: pairs
Row 1: 3 ch to turn, the rest in dc
Row 2: 1 ch to turn, sc for the rest of the row
Row 3: 2 ch to turn, *1 extended dc, 1 sc*
Row 4: 1 ch to turn, sc for the rest of the row
After rows 1–4, keep repeating rows 3 and 4. Row 3 is the right side of the piece.

VARIANT

For looser patterns, replace the single crochets with half double crochets and the double crochets in row 1, and extended ones in row 3 onward with double treble crochets.

TECHNIQUE

1. The first two rows are preparatory and are not repeated. Make 1 row of double crochets, then 1 row of single crochets ▼. The double crochets in row 1 will support the extended double crochets in row 3.

Tip

For orientation, the extended double crochets are vertically aligned and made on the right side of the piece.

¤

2. In row 3, make 2 chain stitches to turn, and then alternate 1 extended double crochet and 1 single crochet over the rest of the row.

3▲ To make the extended double crochet, yarn over once, and insert the hook around the back of the double crochet 2 rows below. Yarn over, draw through 2 loops, yarn over again, and thread the yarn through the remaining 2 stitches. In row 4, make 1 chain stitch to turn, single crochet for the rest of the row.

Bobble Stitch

The succession of yarn overs and stitches drawn together forms little balls the size of hazelnuts.

EQUIPMENT

- crochet hook
- yarn

USES

- accessories
- borders
- main body

STITCHES USED

- single crochet
- double crochet

THE STITCH

Number of Stitches: multiples of 3 sts +1

Row 1: all in sc

Row 2: 1 ch to turn, 1 sc, *x5 in 1 same st (1 yarn over, insert hook under the top stitch, 1 yarn over, pull 1 loop, 1 yarn over, draw through 2 loops), 1 yarn over, draw through 6 loops, 2 sc*

Row 3: all in sc

Row 4: 1 ch to turn, 2 sc, *x5 in 1 same st (1 yarn over, insert hook under the top stitch, 1 yarn over, pull 1 loop, 1 yarn over, draw through 2 loops), 1 yarn over, draw through 6 loops, 2 sc*

Repeat these 4 rows as many times as needed. Row 1 represents the right side of the piece.

TECHNIQUE

1▼ In rows 2 and 4, the bobbles are formed on the wrong side with a series of double crochets. Repeat 5 times in the same stitch: 1 yarn over, insert the hook under the top stitch, 1 yarn over, pull 1 loop, 1 yarn over, pass the yarn through 2 stitches. With each turn, you'll add 1 extra stitch to the hook.

2▲ At the end of the fifth row, you'll have 6 stitches on your hook. Yarn over and thread the yarn through the 6 stitches. Make 2 single crochets and then move on to the next bobble.

Tip

For orientation, the bobbles are always made on the wrong side of the piece and are offset by two stitches.

¤

Ball Stitch

Forming little pouches, the ball stitch is one of the most striking relief stitches.

EQUIPMENT

- crochet hook
- yarn

USES

- accessories
- main body

STITCHES USED

- single crochet
- double crochet
- chain stitch

THE STITCH

Number of Stitches: multiples of 6 sts +5

Rows 1–3: 1 ch to turn, sc for the rest of the rw

Row 4: 1 ch to turn, 5 sc, *1 ch, 6 dc inserted under the same sc in the rw before last, remove the hook from the st, insert it under the last ch and pass the loose st through, 5 sc*

Rows 5–7: 1 ch to turn, sc for the rest of the rw

Row 8: 1 ch to turn, 2 sc, *1 ch, 6 dc inserted under the same sc in the rw before last, remove the hook from the st, insert it under the last ch and pass the loose st through, 5 sc,* 3 sc
Repeat these eight rows as many times as needed.

TECHNIQUE

1▼ To create a ball, make 1 chain stitch and 1 yarn over. Insert the hook under the single crochet in the row before last and make a double crochet.

2. Make 5 more double crochets, always inserted into the same stitch in the row before last.

3▲ Remove the hook from the stitch, and insert it into the chain stitch. Hook the loose stitch and pull it through the chain stitch to seal the ball.

Tip

Balls are made in one single crochet but can span two. To keep the same number of stitches, insert the hook into the stitch that seals the ball in the next row twice.

¤

Border
Stitches

Picot Stitch

Generally delicate and understated, the picots resemble the little teeth in lace.

EQUIPMENT

- crochet hook
- yarn

USES

- borders

STITCHES USED

- single crochet
- chain stitch
- slip stitch

THE STITCH

Number of Stitches: multiples of 3 sts
Row 1: *2 sl st, 1 sc, 5 ch, 1 sl st inserted into the sc*

VARIANTS

For smaller picots, make 3 ch instead of 5. Then make 1 sl st in the 1st ch.
For double crochet picots separated by single crochets, carry out the following steps.
Number of Stitches: multiples of 8 sts
Row 1: *6 sc, in 1 same st (1 dc, 1 picot of 3 ch) x3, then 1 dc*
The larger the picots, the more they need to be separated by several slip stitches.

TECHNIQUE

1▼ Repeat for the entire row: 2 slip stitches, 1 single crochet . . .

3▲ To secure the picot, make 1 slip stitch inserted into the previous single crochet.

2▼ . . . and 5 chain stitches.

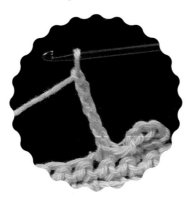

Tip

For orientation, the picots are separated by two slip stitches. These subtle stitches emphasize the picots.

¤

Palm Arches

The radial pattern of the double crochets forms a palm-like shape attached to small arches.

EQUIPMENT

- crochet hook
- yarn

USES

- borders

STITCHES USED

- double crochet
- chain stitch
- single crochet

THE STITCH

Number of Stitches: multiples of 4
sts +1
Row 1: *1 sc, 3 ch, skip 3 sts,* 1 sc
Row 2: 1 sc, *7 dc under the 3 ch in the
prev rw, 1 sc*

TECHNIQUE

1▼ This border is made up of 2 rows.
In row 1, repeat: 1 single crochet, 3
chain stitches, and skip 3
stitches. Finish the row with 1
single crochet.

2▲ For row 2, make 1 single crochet,
then repeat the following steps: 7
double crochets inserted under
the chain stitches in the previous
row, and 1 single crochet inserted
under the top stitch of the single
crochet in the previous row.

Tip

The seven double crochets, made
under the three chain stitches,
are tight and add relief to the
palms. Avoid overlapping them.

¤

Shell Stitch

This decorative shell design is formed from several double crochets made in the same stitch.

EQUIPMENT

- crochet hook
- yarn

USES

- borders

STITCHES USED

- slip stitch
- double crochet

THE STITCH

Number of Stitches: multiples of 4 sts +1

Row 1: 1 sl st, *skip 2 sts, 5 dc in 1 st, skip 2 sts, 1 sl st*

VARIANT

For larger shells, work on multiples of 8 sts +1.

Row 1: 1 sl st, *skip 3 sts, 8 tr in 1 st, skip 3 sts, 1 sl st*

TECHNIQUE

1▼ This border is made with just one row. Make 1 slip stitch, then repeat the following steps: Skip 2 stitches and, in the next stitch, make 5 double crochets.

2▲ Then skip 2 stitches and make 1 slip stitch. Continue like this to the end of the row.

Tip

The double crochets need room to expand and form the shell, so you need to skip two stitches between each motif.

¤

Clover Stitch

This simple three-circle shape is created by a variation of the chain stitch.

EQUIPMENT

- crochet hook
- yarn

USES

- borders

STITCHES USED

- single crochet
- chain stitch
- slip stitch

THE STITCH

Number of Stitches: multiples of 5 sts +1
Row 1: 1 ch, skip 1 st, *in 1 st (1 sc, 3 ch, 1 sl st), in the nxt st (1 sc, 5 ch, 1 sl st), in the nxt st (1 sc, 3 ch, 1 sl st), 2 sc*

VARIANT

For larger foliage, simply increase the number of chain stitches in proportion to the size wanted.
Row 1: 1 ch, skip 1 st, *in 1 st (1 sc, 5 ch, 1 sl st), in the nxt st (1 sc, 7 ch, 1 sl st), in the nxt st (1 sc, 5 ch, 1 sl st), 2 sc*

TECHNIQUE

1. Make 1 chain stitch to turn, skip 1 stitch, and repeat the following steps: Insert the hook under the next top stitch and make 1 single crochet, 3 chain stitches, and 1 slip stitch inserted into the previous single crochet ▼.

2▲ In the next stitch, do the same steps with 5 chain stitches. Then, in the next stitch, do the same as in step 1 with 3 chain stitches.

Tip

The clovers are separated by two single crochets. If you want to loosen them further, replace the single crochets with slip stitches.

¤

Wavy Shell Stitch

Reminiscent of serrated edging, these small ridges are created by successively crossing double crochets.

EQUIPMENT

- crochet hook
- yarn

USES

- borders

STITCHES USED

- chain stitch
- double crochet
- slip stitch

ESSENTIAL CROCHET DICTIONARY

THE STITCH

Number of Stitches: multiples of 4 sts +4

Row 1: 3 ch to turn, skip 3 sts, *1 dc, 3 ch, 4 dc inserted around the prev dc, skip 3 sts,* 3 ch, 1 sl st

VARIANT

For larger ridges, replace the double crochets with treble crochets.

Number of Stitches: multiples of 5 sts +5

Row 1: 5 ch to turn, skip 4 sts, *1 tr, 5 ch, 6 tr inserted around the prev tr, skip 4 sts,* 5 ch, 1 sl st

TECHNIQUE

1▼ This motif is made with just one row. Make 3 chain stitches to turn, skip 3 stitches, then repeat the following steps: Make 1 double crochet and 3 chain stitches.

2▲ To form a ridge, make 4 double crochets by inserting the hook around the previous double crochet. Skip 3 stitches.

3. Finish the row with 3 chain stitches, skip 3 stitches, and a slip stitch in the last stitch.

Tip

For orientation, the double crochet that supports the four double crochets forming the ridge is always separated from the next by three skipped stitches.

Wavy Stitch

The use of different basic stitches, ranging from small to large, creates a decorative wave effect that's easy to achieve.

EQUIPMENT

- crochet hook
- yarn

USES

- sleeve edges
- borders

STITCHES USED

- single crochet
- double crochet
- half double crochet

THE STITCH

Number of Stitches: multiples of 8 sts +1

Row 1: 1 sl st, *1 sc, 1 hdc, 1 dc, 1 tr, 1 dc, 1 hdc, 1 sc, 1 sl st*

VARIANT

To increase the width of the wave, work on multiples of 11 sts +1.

Row 1: 1 sl st, *1 sc, 1 hdc, 1 dc, 1 tr, 2 dtr, 1 tr, 1 dc, 1 hdc, 1 sc, 1 sl st*

TECHNIQUE

1▼ This motif is made with just one row. Start with 1 slip stitch, then repeat the following steps: 1 single crochet, 1 half double crochet, 1 double crochet, 1 treble crochet. This last stitch is the peak of the wave.

2▲ Continue with 1 double crochet, 1 half double crochet, 1 single crochet, and 1 slip stitch.

Tip

For orientation, the waves are separated by a slip stitch, which marks the lowest point.

¤

Picot Cone Stitch

Wrapped around the double treble crochet, the stitches form a cone topped by a picot.

EQUIPMENT

- crochet hook
- yarn

USES

- trim

STITCHES USED

- chain stitch
- single crochet
- half double crochet
- double crochet
- treble crochet
- double treble crochet

THE STITCH

Number of Stitches: multiples of 5 sts +1

Row 1: 1 ch to turn, sc for the rest of the rw

Row 2: 1 ch to turn, sc for the rest of the row

Row 3: 1 ch to turn, *2 sc, 3 picots (4 ch, 1 sl st on the 1st ch), 1 dtr, (1 sc, 1 hdc, 1 dc, 1 tr) inserted around the prev dtr, skip 2 sts,* 1 sc

Tip

The four stitches made in the double treble crochet are in ascending order to form the cone: one single crochet, one half double crochet, one double crochet, one treble crochet. Avoid overlapping them.

¤

TECHNIQUE

1. Make two rows of single crochets with 1 chain stitch to turn.

2▼ For row 3, make 1 chain stitch to turn, then repeat the following steps: 2 single crochets and 3 picots. To create a picot, make 4 chain stitches, then insert the hook into the first chain stitch, and make 1 slip stitch. The 3 picots follow one another.

3▼ Continue with 1 double treble crochet inserted under the next top stitch. Going around this double treble crochet, make 1 single crochet, 1 half double crochet, 1 double crochet, and 1 treble crochet.

4. Skip 2 stitches to move onto the next cone. Finish the row with 1 single crochet.

Flower Border Stitch

Placed in a staggered pattern, the series of radiating double crochets resemble a succession of small roses.

EQUIPMENT

- crochet hook
- yarn

USES

- trim

STITCHES USED

- chain stitch
- double crochet
- half double crochet

ESSENTIAL CROCHET DICTIONARY

THE STITCH

Number of Stitches: 3 sts
Row 1: in the 1st st (2 hdc, 2 ch, 2 hdc), 2 ch, *under the ch in the prev group of hdc (2 hdc, 2 ch, 2 hdc), 2 ch*

VARIANT

For larger flowers, replace the half double crochets with double crochets as follows.
Row 1: in the 1st st (3 dc, 3 ch, 3 dc), 3 ch, *under the ch in the prev group of dc (3 dc, 3 ch, 3 dc), 3 ch*

TECHNIQUE

1▼ The 3 chain stitches are the starting point for the first flower. In the first stitch, make 2 half double crochets, 2 chain stitches, and 2 more half double crochets. The 2 chain stitches will be the starting point for a new flower.

2▲ Insert the hook under these chain stitches and make 2 half double crochets, 2 chain stitches, and 2 more half double crochets. Continue by repeating these steps.

Tip

For orientation, the flowers are attached to the previous chain stitches and positioned alternately on either side of the trim.

¤

Half-Daisy Border Stitch

This very simple trim is made up of a series of three floral buds.

EQUIPMENT

- crochet hook
- yarn

USES

- trim

STITCHES USED

- chain stitch
- double crochet
- half double crochet

THE STITCH

Number of Stitches: multiples of 8 sts +1

Row 1: 2 ch to turn, the rest in hdc
Row 2: 1 ch to turn, 1 sc, *2 ch, skip 2 sts, in 1 st x3 (1 yarn over, insert, 1 yarn over, pull 1 loop), 1 yarn over, draw through all the loops, 2 ch, in 1 st x3 (1 yarn over, insert, 1 yarn over, pull 1 loop), 1 yarn over, draw through all the loops, 2 ch, in 1 st x3 (1 yarn over, insert, 1 yarn over, pull 1 loop), 1 yarn over, draw through all the loops, 2 ch, skip 2 sts, 1 sc*

TECHNIQUE

1. Make a first row of half double crochets with 2 chain stitches to turn.
2.▼ For row 2, make 1 chain stitch to turn, and 1 single crochet. Then repeat the following steps: 2 chain stitches and skip 2 stitches. In the next stitch, create a flower by repeating 3 times: 1 yarn over, insert, 1 yarn over, pull 1 loop. You'll now have 7 loops on your hook.

3.▲ Yarn over and thread the yarn through the 7 loops to seal the flower. Make 2 more flowers separated by 2 chain stitches.
4. Continue with 2 chain stitches, skip 2 stitches, and a single crochet. Repeat these steps to make the next group of flowers.

Tip

The flowers are grouped in threes, separated by two chain stitches. Each group is spaced five stitches apart, with one single crochet on the third.

¤

Crown Stitch

A series of double crochets attached to little arches and topped with picots remind us of the royal insignia of power.

EQUIPMENT

- crochet hook
- yarn

USES

- trim

STITCHES USED

- single crochet
- slip stitch
- chain stitch
- double crochet

ESSENTIAL CROCHET DICTIONARY

THE STITCH

Number of Stitches: multiples of 7 sts +1

Row 1: 1 ch to turn, sc for the rest of the rw

Row 2: 1 ch to turn, *1 sc, 2 ch, skip 2 sts, 1 dc, 4 ch, 1 dc, 2 ch, skip 2 sts,* 1 sc

Row 3: 2 ch to turn, *under each 4 ch in the prev rw (4 dc, 3 picots of 4 ch, 4 dc),* 1 sc

Tip

For orientation, the crowns are made up of two groups of four double crochets topped by three picots.

¤

TECHNIQUE

1. Make 1 chain stitch to turn, and then continue with single crochets for the rest of the row.
2. For row 2, make 1 chain stitch to turn, then repeat the following steps: 1 single crochet, 2 chain stitches, skip 2 stitches, 1 double crochet ▼, 4 chain stitches, 1 double crochet, 2 chain stitches, and skip 2 stitches. Finish the row with 1 single crochet.

3. For row 3, make 2 chain stitches to turn, and repeat the following inserted into each group of 4 chain stitches in the previous row: 4 double crochets, 3 picots, and 4 double crochets. Finish with 1 single crochet.

4▲ For each picot, make 4 chain stitches. Secure with 1 slip stitch inserted in the first of these chain stitches.

Flora Tiara Stitch

Several double crochets joined together form the petals of a flower arranged in a crown.

EQUIPMENT

- crochet hook
- yarn

USES

- trim

STITCHES USED

- single crochet
- half double crochet
- treble crochet
- chain stitch

THE STITCH

Number of Stitches: multiples of 8 sts +5

Row 1: 2 ch to turn, hdc for the rest of the rw

Row 2: 1 ch to turn, 5 sc, *5 ch, skip 3 sts, 5 sc*

Row 3: 3 ch to turn, *under each ch arch in the prev rw (3 tr without drawing through the last st, 1 yarn over, draw through 3 loops, 1 yarn over, draw through 2 loops), repeat 3 times at intervals of 3 ch,* 3 ch, 1 sc in the last st

Tip

When starting a new arch, tighten the first double crochet to avoid creating an unsightly gap between it and the previous set of double crochets.

¤

TECHNIQUE

1. For row 1, make 2 chain stitches to turn, then continue with half double crochets.
2. For row 2, make 1 chain stitch to turn, and 5 single crochets, then repeat: 5 chain stitches, skip 3 stitches, and 5 single crochets.

You'll now have 4 stitches on your hook.

4▲ Yarn over once, draw through 3 loops, 1 yarn over, draw through 2 loops. Make 3 chain stitches, then repeat the group of 3 double crochets two more times.

5. Now repeat for each chain stitch arch. The 3 x 3 double crochets joined together are separated by 3 chain stitches. Finish the row with 3 chain stitches and a single crochet in the last stitch.

3▲ For row 3, make 3 chain stitches to turn, then under the chain stitch arch in the previous row, make 3 treble crochets without drawing through the last stitch.

Tunisian Stitches

Simple Tunisian Stitch

This dense, full pattern is the basis for most Tunisian crochet stitches and features a tight, perfectly uniform grid.

EQUIPMENT

- Tunisian crochet hook
- yarn

USES

- accessories
- main body

STITCH USED

- simple Tunisian stitch

THE STITCH

Number of Stitches: any

Row 1: 1 ch to turn, *1 yarn over, insert under the st, pull 1 loop*

Row 2: 1 ch to turn, *1 yarn over, draw through 2 loops*

Repeat these 2 rows as many times as needed.

TECHNIQUE

1▼ For row 1, make 1 chain stitch to turn, and work from right to left. Insert the hook under the vertical loop, yarn over once, and pull 1 loop. Continue like this to the end of the row. All the loops are kept on the hook.

2▲ For row 2, make 1 chain stitch to return. Repeat the following steps across the whole row, working from left to right (the hook moves backward): Yarn over and draw through 2 loops.

Tip

At the end of the row on the forward pass, the hook is inserted under the stitch that forms the selvage to complete the row. The expression "to turn" implies "forward" or "return." Do not turn the piece over.

¤

Twisted Simple Tunisian Stitch

Based on the simple Tunisian stitch, the twisted simple stitch involves adding a chain stitch to each crochet stitch.

EQUIPMENT

- Tunisian crochet hook
- yarn

USES

- accessories
- main body

STITCHES USED

- simple Tunisian stitch
- chain stitch

ESSENTIAL CROCHET DICTIONARY

THE STITCH

Number of Stitches: any
Row 1: 1 ch to turn, simple stitch for the rest of the rw
Row 2: 1 ch to turn, simple stitch for the rest of the row
Row 3: *insert under the vertical loop, 1 yarn over, draw through 1 loop, 1 ch*
Row 4: 1 ch to turn, simple stitch for the rest of the row
After rows 1–4, keep repeating rows 3 and 4.

VARIANT

In row 3, instead of inserting the hook under the vertical loop, insert it between 2 vertical loops, then yarn over once, draw through 1 loop, and make 1 chain stitch.

TECHNIQUE

1. For rows 1 and 4, make 1 chain stitch to turn and repeat the following to the end of the row: Insert the hook under the vertical loop, yarn over, and pull 1 loop. Keep all the loops on the hook.

2▼ For row 2, make 1 chain stitch to return, then repeat the following to the end of the row: Yarn over and draw through 2 loops.

3▲ For row 3, make 1 chain stitch to turn, then repeat the following steps: Insert the hook under the vertical loop and do the following twice (yarn over, pull 1 loop). The second yarn over and the loop are the same as a chain stitch.

Tip

This stitch is more flexible and less compact, and it can be completed more quickly than the simple stitch.

¤

Extended Tunisian Knit Stitch

Similar to the simple stitch in its compactness, the extended knit stitch looks a bit like a honeycomb.

EQUIPMENT

- Tunisian crochet hook
- yarn

USES

- accessories
- main body

STITCH USED

- simple Tunisian stitch

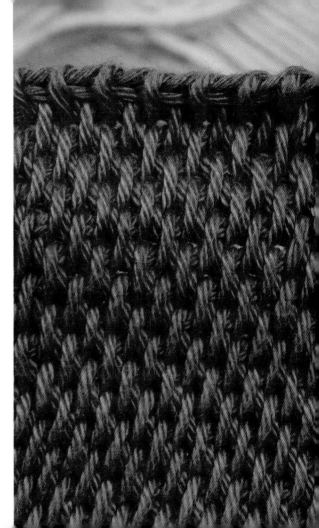

THE STITCH

Number of Stitches: pairs

Row 1: 1 ch to turn, simple stitch for the rest of the rw

Row 2: 1 ch to turn, simple stitch for the rest of the rw

Row 3: 1 ch to turn, *insert between the 2 vertical loops, 1 yarn over, and pull 1 loop,* insert under the selvage ch and pull 1 loop

After rows 1–3, keep repeating rows 2 and 3.

Tip

For orientation, the loops are vertically aligned. The pattern forms ridged diagonal lines.

¤

TECHNIQUE

1. For row 1, make 1 chain stitch to turn, and repeat the following to the end of the row: Insert the hook under the vertical loop, yarn over, and pull 1 loop. Keep all the loops on the hook.

2▼ For row 2, make 1 chain stitch to return, then repeat the following to the end of the row: Yarn over and draw through 2 loops.

3▲ For row 3, make 1 chain stitch to turn, and repeat the following to the end of the row: Insert the hook between the 2 vertical loops, yarn over, and pull 1 loop. Keep all the loops on the hook. At the end of the row, insert the hook under the selvage stitch, yarn over, and pull 1 loop.

Tunisian Mesh Stitch

A skipped stitch gives this stitch an airy, trellis-like appearance.

EQUIPMENT

- Tunisian crochet hook
- yarn

USES

- accessories
- main body

STITCH USED

- simple Tunisian stitch

THE STITCH

Number of Stitches: multiples of 2 sts +3

Row 1: 1 ch to turn, 1 yarn over, skip 2 sts, insert and pull 1 loop, *1 yarn over, skip 1 st, insert, 1 yarn over, pull 1 loop*

Row 2: 1 ch to turn, simple stitch for the rest of the rw

Row 3: 1 ch to turn, *1 yarn over, insert under the first st, 1 yarn over, pull 1 loop*

Row 4: 1 ch to turn, simple stitch for the rest of the row

After rows 1–4, keep repeating rows 3 and 4.

TECHNIQUE

1▼ For row 1, make 1 chain stitch to turn, yarn over, skip 2 stitches, and insert the hook under the vertical loop, and pull 1 loop. Then repeat for the entire row: 1 yarn over, skip 1 stitch, insert the hook, 1 yarn over, pull 1 loop.

2. For row 2, make 2 chain stitches to turn and repeat: Yarn over and draw through 2 loops.

3▲ For row 3, make 2 chain stitches to turn and repeat: Yarn over, insert the hook under the second stitch, yarn over again, and pull 1 loop.

4. For row 4, make 1 chain stitch to turn and repeat the following: Yarn over, draw through 2 loops.

Tip

For orientation, in row 3, the skipped stitch is the one created by the yarn over in the previous row.

¤

Tunisian Shell Stitch

Sometimes called "Tunisian lace," this stitch combines several stitches to create openwork.

EQUIPMENT

- Tunisian crochet hook
- yarn

USES

- accessories
- main body

STITCH USED

- simple Tunisian stitch

THE STITCH

Number of Stitches: pairs

Row 1: 1 ch to turn, simple stitch for the rest of the rw

Row 2: 1 ch to turn, simple stitch for the rest of the rw

Row 3: 1 ch to turn, simple stitch for the rest of the rw

Row 4: 3 ch, *1 yarn over, draw through 5 loops, 4 ch,* 1 yarn over, draw through 5 loops, 1 ch, 1 yarn over, draw through 2 loops

Row 5: 1 ch to turn, x2 (1 yarn over, draw through 1 loop), *in each of the 4 ch (1 yarn over, draw through 1 loop),* in each of the 3 ch (1 yarn over, draw through 1 loop)

After rows 1–5, keep repeating rows 4 and 5.

TECHNIQUE

1. Rows 1–3 represent 1 forward, 1 return, and 1 forward in simple stitch with 1 chain stitch to turn.

2▼ For row 4, make 3 chain stitches to return and then repeat: Yarn over, draw through 5 loops, 4 chain stitches.

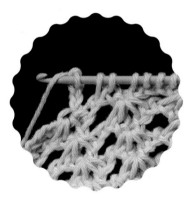

3. Finish the row with 1 yarn over, draw through 5 loops, 1 chain stitch, 1 yarn over, and draw through the 2 last loops.

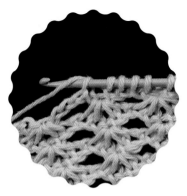

4▲ For row 5, make 1 chain stitch to turn, and repeat the following twice (yarn over, draw through 1 loop). Then repeat (1 yarn over, draw through 1 loop) in each of the 4 chain stitches. Finish with (1 yarn over, draw through 1 loop) in each of the 3 end stitches.

Tip

The four-chain stitch arches are vertically aligned and, in row 3, represent four stitches.

¤

Tunisian Cross Stitch

This slightly open stitch creates an alignment of small crosses as a result of the two stitches crocheted together.

EQUIPMENT

- Tunisian crochet hook
- yarn

USES

- accessories
- main body

STITCH USED

- simple Tunisian stitch

THE STITCH

Number of Stitches: multiples of 2 sts
Row 1: 1 ch to turn, simple stitch for the rest of the rw
Row 2: 1 ch to turn, simple stitch for the rest of the rw
Row 3: 1 ch to turn, *insert under 2 loops, 1 yarn over, draw through 1 loop, insert under 1 ch, 1 yarn over, draw through 1 loop*
After rows 1–3, keep repeating rows 2 and 3.

TECHNIQUE

1. For row 1, make 1 chain stitch to turn, and repeat the following to the end of the row: Insert the hook under the vertical loop, yarn over, and pull 1 loop. Keep all the loops on the hook.
2. For row 2, make 1 chain stitch to return, then repeat the following to the end of the row: Yarn over and draw through 2 loops.

3▲ For row 3, make 1 chain stitch to turn, then repeat the following steps: Insert the hook under 2 vertical loops, yarn over, draw through 1 loop.
4◀ Then insert the hook into the chain stitch located just before the next vertical loop, yarn over once, and draw through 1 loop. Continue like this to the end of the row.

Tip

For orientation, in row 3, the stitches are arranged in pairs on the hook. The pattern openings are located between each group of two stitches.

¤

Index

Stitches are classified here according to the different types of stitch used. Once you've mastered a stitch, you can easily tackle any pattern that uses it. However, several stitch types may be combined in a single stitch pattern.

Crochet Hook Sizes

Millimeter Size	US Label
2.25mm	B-1
2.75mm	C-2
3.25mm	D-3
3.5mm	E-4
3.75mm	F-5
4mm	G-6
4.5mm	7
5mm	H-8
5.5mm	I-9
6mm	J-10
6.5mm	K-10 1/2
8mm	L-11
9mm	M/N-13
10mm	N/P-15
11.5mm	P-16
15mm	P/Q
16mm	Q